Oscar

WHERE'S WALLY?

THE ULTIMATE TRAVEL COLLECTION

MARTIN HANDFORD

WALKER BOOKS
AND SUBSIDIARIES
LONDON · BOSTON · SYDNEY · AUCKLAND

HI WALLY-WATCHER!

ARE YOU READY TO JOIN ME ON MY FIVE
FANTASTIC ADVENTURES?

WHERE'S WALLY?
WHERE'S WALLY NOW?
WHERE'S WALLY? THE FANTASTIC JOURNEY
WHERE'S WALLY? IN HOLLYWOOD
WHERE'S WALLY? THE WONDER BOOK

CAN YOU FIND THE FIVE INTREPID TRAVELLERS
AND THEIR PRECIOUS ITEMS IN EVERY SCENE?

ODLAW   WIZARD   WENDA   WOOF   WALLY
         WHITEBEARD

 WALLY'S KEY   WOOF'S BONE   WENDA'S CAMERA

 WIZARD WHITEBEARD'S
SCROLL   ODLAW'S BINOCULARS

WAIT, THERE'S MORE! AT THE BEGINNING AND
END OF EACH ADVENTURE, FIND A FOLD-OUT
CHECKLIST WITH HUNDREDS MORE THINGS TO
LOOK FOR.

WOW! WHAT A SEARCH!

BON VOYAGE!

Wally

WHERE'S RAILWAY STATION WALLY?

WHERE'S CAMP SITE WALLY?

WHERE'S SKI SLOPES WALLY?

WHERE'S AIRPORT WALLY?

WHERE'S SPORTS STADIUM WALLY?

WHERE'S MUSEUM WALLY?

WHERE'S AT SEA WALLY?

SAFARI PARK WHERE'S WALLY?

WHERE'S ON THE BEACH WALLY?

WHERE'S WALLY?

HI FRIENDS!

MY NAME IS WALLY. I'M JUST SETTING OFF ON A WORLD-WIDE HIKE. YOU CAN COME TOO. ALL YOU HAVE TO DO IS FIND ME.

I'VE GOT ALL I NEED – WALKING STICK, KETTLE, MALLET, CUP, RUCKSACK, SLEEPING BAG, BINOCULARS, CAMERA, SNORKEL, BELT, BAG AND SHOVEL.

BY THE WAY, I'M NOT TRAVELLING ON MY OWN. WHEREVER I GO, THERE ARE LOTS OF OTHER CHARACTERS FOR YOU TO SPOT. FIRST FIND WOOF (BUT ALL YOU CAN SEE IS HIS TAIL), WENDA, WIZARD WHITEBEARD AND ODLAW. THERE ARE ALSO 25 WALLY-WATCHERS SOMEWHERE, EACH OF WHOM APPEARS ONLY ONCE ON MY TRAVELS. CAN YOU FIND ONE OTHER CHARACTER WHO APPEARS IN EVERY SCENE? ALSO IN EVERY SCENE, CAN YOU SPOT WIZARD WHITEBEARD'S SCROLL, MY KEY, WOOF'S BONE, WENDA'S CAMERA, AND ODLAW'S BINOCULARS?

WOW! WHAT A SEARCH!

Wally

THE GREAT WHERE'S WALLY? CHECKLIST: PART ONE

Hundreds of things for Wally-watchers to watch out for! Don't forget PART TWO at the end of this adventure!

IN TOWN

- A dog on a roof
- A man on a fountain
- A man about to trip over a dog's lead
- A car crash
- A keen barber
- People in a street, watching TV
- A puncture caused by a Roman arrow
- A tearful tune
- A boy attacked by a plant
- A waiter who isn't concentrating
- A robber who's been clobbered
- A face on a wall
- A man coming out of a man-hole
- A man feeding pigeons
- A bicycle crash

ON THE BEACH

- A dog biting a boy's bottom
- A man who is overdressed
- A muscular medallion man
- A popular girl
- A water skier on water
- A stripy photo
- A punctured lilo
- A donkey who likes ice-cream
- A man being squashed
- A punctured beach ball
- A human pyramid
- A human stepping-stone
- Two odd friends
- A cowboy
- A human donkey
- Age and beauty
- A boy who follows in his father's footsteps
- Two men with vests, one without
- A boy being tortured by a spider
- A show-off with sand castles
- A gang of hat robbers
- An Arab making pyramids
- Three protruding tongues
- Two oddly fitting hats
- An odd couple
- Five sprinters
- A towel with a hole in it
- A punctured hovercraft
- A boy who's not allowed any ice-cream

SKI SLOPES

- A man reading on a roof
- A flying skier
- A runaway skier
- A backward skier
- A portrait in snow
- An illegal fisherman
- A snowball in the neck
- Two unconscious skiers
- Two skiers hitting trees
- An Alpine horn
- A snow skier
- A flag collector
- Two very scruffy skiers
- A skier up a tree
- A water-skier on snow
- A Yeti
- A skiing reindeer
- A roof jumper
- A heap of skaters

CAMPSITE

- A bull in a hedge
- Bull horns
- A shark in a canal
- A bull seeing red
- A careless kick
- Tea in a lap
- A low bridge
- People knocked over by a mallet
- A man surprised undressing
- A bicycle tyre about to be punctured
- Camper's camels
- A scarecrow that doesn't work
- A wigwam
- Large biceps
- A collapsed tent
- A smoking barbecue
- A fisherman catching old boots
- A winning penny-farthing
- Boy Scouts making fire
- A roller hiker
- A man blowing up a boat
- A camper's butler
- Runners on the road
- A bull chasing children
- Scruffy campers
- Thirsty walkers

THE RAILWAY STATION

- A boy falling from a train
- A break-down on tracks
- Naughty children on a train roof
- People being knocked over by a door
- A man about to step on a ball
- Three different times at the same time
- A wheelbarrow pram
- A face on a train
- Five people reading one newspaper
- A struggling bag carrier
- A show-off with suitcases
- A man losing everything from his cases
- A smoking train
- A squeeze on a bench
- A dog tearing a man's trousers
- Fare dodgers
- A hand caught between doors
- A cattle stampede
- A man breaking a weighing machine

AIRPORT

- A flying saucer
- A boy who's been hiding in a suitcase
- A child firing a catapult
- A leaking fuel pipe
- Flight controllers playing badminton
- A rocket
- A turret
- Three watch smugglers
- Naughty children on a plane
- A forklift truck
- A wind-sock
- A chopper
- A plane that doesn't fly
- A flying Ace
- Dracula
- Five men blowing up a balloon
- Runners on a runaway
- Four smoking people
- Four people falling from a plane
- A cargo of cattle
- A fire engine
- Three childish pilots
- An airship being punctured

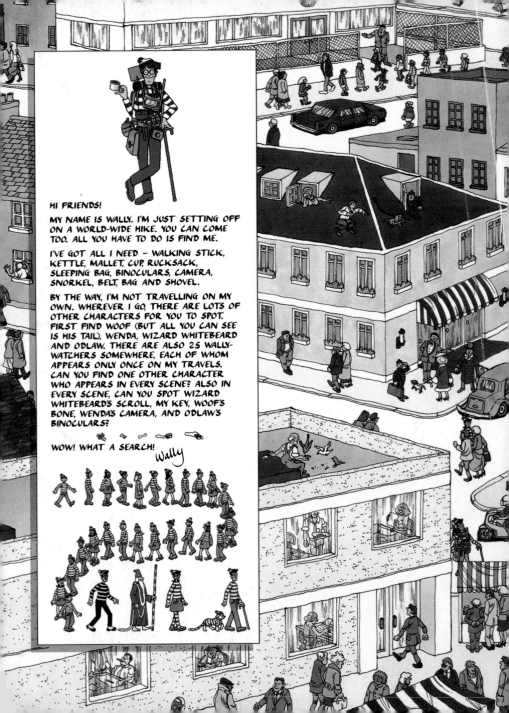

HI FRIENDS!

MY NAME IS WALLY. I'M JUST SETTING OFF ON A WORLD-WIDE HIKE. YOU CAN COME TOO. ALL YOU HAVE TO DO IS FIND ME.

I'VE GOT ALL I NEED – WALKING STICK, KETTLE, MALLET, CUP, RUCKSACK, SLEEPING BAG, BINOCULARS, CAMERA, SNORKEL, BELT, BAG AND SHOVEL.

BY THE WAY, I'M NOT TRAVELLING ON MY OWN. WHEREVER I GO, THERE ARE LOTS OF OTHER CHARACTERS FOR YOU TO SPOT. FIRST FIND WOOF (BUT ALL YOU CAN SEE IS HIS TAIL), WENDA, WIZARD WHITEBEARD AND ODLAW. THERE ARE ALSO 25 WALLY-WATCHERS SOMEWHERE, EACH OF WHOM APPEARS ONLY ONCE ON MY TRAVELS. CAN YOU FIND ONE OTHER CHARACTER WHO APPEARS IN EVERY SCENE? ALSO IN EVERY SCENE, CAN YOU SPOT WIZARD WHITEBEARD'S SCROLL, MY KEY, WOOF'S BONE, WENDA'S CAMERA, AND ODLAW'S BINOCULARS?

WOW! WHAT A SEARCH!

Wally

GREETINGS,
WALLY FOLLOWERS!
WOW, THE BEACH WAS
GREAT TODAY! I SAW
THIS GIRL STICK AN
ICE-CREAM IN HER
BROTHER'S FACE, AND
THERE WAS A SAND-
CASTLE WITH A REAL
KNIGHT IN ARMOUR
INSIDE! FANTASTIC!

Wally

TO:
WALLY FOLLOWERS,
HERE, THERE,
EVERYWHERE.

WHERE'S
ON THE BEACH
WALLY?

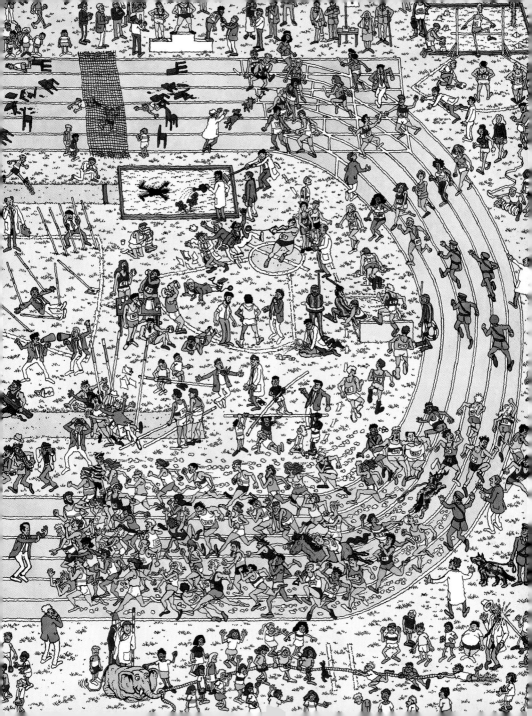

THE GREAT WHERE'S WALLY?
CHECKLIST: PART TWO

SPORTS STADIUM

- [ ] Three pairs of feet, sticking out of sand
- [ ] A cowboy starting races
- [ ] Hopeless hurdlers
- [ ] Ten children with fifteen legs
- [ ] A record thrower
- [ ] A shot-put juggler
- [ ] An ear trumpet
- [ ] A vaulting horse
- [ ] A runner with two wheels
- [ ] A parachuting vaulter
- [ ] A Scotsman with a caber
- [ ] An elephant pulling a rope
- [ ] People being knocked over by a hammer
- [ ] A gardener
- [ ] Three frogmen
- [ ] A runner without any shorts on
- [ ] A bed
- [ ] A bandaged boy
- [ ] A runner with four legs
- [ ] A sunken jumper
- [ ] A man with an odd pair of legs
- [ ] A man chasing a dog chasing a cat
- [ ] A boy squirting water

MUSEUM

- [ ] A very big skeleton
- [ ] A clown squirting water
- [ ] A catapult firing a child
- [ ] A bird's nest in a woman's hair
- [ ] A highwayman
- [ ] A popping bicep
- [ ] An arrow in the neck
- [ ] A knight watching TV
- [ ] Picture robbers
- [ ] A smoking picture
- [ ] A leaking watercolour
- [ ] Fighting pictures
- [ ] A king and queen
- [ ] A fat picture and a thin one
- [ ] Three cave men
- [ ] A game of catch with a bomb
- [ ] Charioteers
- [ ] A collapsing pillar

AT SEA

- [ ] A windsurfer
- [ ] A boat punctured by an arrow
- [ ] A sword fight with a swordfish
- [ ] A school of whales
- [ ] Seasick sailors
- [ ] A leaking diver
- [ ] A boat crash
- [ ] A bathtub
- [ ] A seabed
- [ ] A game of noughts and crosses
- [ ] A lucky fisherman
- [ ] Three lumberjacks
- [ ] Unlucky fishermen
- [ ] Two water skiers in a tangle
- [ ] Fish robbers
- [ ] A sea cowboy
- [ ] A fishy photo
- [ ] A man being strangled by an octopus
- [ ] Stowaways
- [ ] A Chinese junk
- [ ] A wave at sea

SAFARI PARK

- [ ] Noah's Ark
- [ ] A message in a bottle
- [ ] A hippo having its teeth cleaned
- [ ] A bird's nest in an antler
- [ ] A hungry giraffe
- [ ] An ice-cream robber
- [ ] A zebra crossing
- [ ] Father Christmas
- [ ] Three owls
- [ ] A unicorn
- [ ] Caged people
- [ ] A lion driving a car
- [ ] Bears
- [ ] Tarzan
- [ ] Lion cubs
- [ ] An Indian tiger
- [ ] Two queues for the toilets
- [ ] Animals' beauty parlour
- [ ] An elephant squirting water

DEPARTMENT STORE

- [ ] An ironing demonstration
- [ ] A woman surprised undressing
- [ ] A man whose boots face the wrong way
- [ ] A man with heavy shopping
- [ ] A misbehaving vacuum cleaner
- [ ] Ties that match their wearers
- [ ] A man washing his clothes
- [ ] A man trying on a jacket that's too big
- [ ] A woman tripping over toys
- [ ] A boy pulling a girl's hair
- [ ] A boy riding in a shopping trolley
- [ ] A glove that's alive

FAIRGROUND

- [ ] A cannon at a rifle range
- [ ] A bumper car run wild
- [ ] A sword swallower
- [ ] A one-armed bandit
- [ ] A flying balloon seller
- [ ] A runaway fairground rocket
- [ ] A runaway fairground horse
- [ ] A haunted house
- [ ] Seven lost children and a lost dog
- [ ] A tank crash
- [ ] A weight lifter dropping his weights
- [ ] Three clowns
- [ ] Three men dressed as bears

WOW! WHAT A SEARCH!

Did you find Wally, all his friends and all the things they lost? Did you find the one scene where Wally and Odlaw both lost their binoculars? Odlaw's binoculars are the ones nearest to him. Did you find the extra character who appears in every scene? If not, keep looking! Wow! Fantastic!

THE ABSOLUTELY HUGE AND ENORMOUSLY INTERESTING BOOK OF CAVEMEN, CAVE WOMEN, CAVE DOGS AND ALL SORTS OF EXTREMELY SAVAGE STONE-AGE BEASTS.

HI THERE, BOOK WORMS!

SOME BITS OF HISTORY ARE AMAZING! I SIT HERE READING ALL THESE BOOKS ABOUT THE WORLD LONG AGO, AND IT'S LIKE RIDING A TIME MACHINE. WHY NOT TRY IT FOR YOURSELVES? JUST SEARCH EACH PICTURE AND FIND ME, WOOF (REMEMBER, ALL YOU CAN SEE IS HIS TAIL), WENDA, WIZARD WHITEBEARD AND ODLAW. THEN LOOK FOR MY KEY, WOOF'S BONE (IN THIS SCENE IT'S THE BONE THAT'S NEAREST TO HIS TAIL), WENDA'S CAMERA, WIZARD WHITEBEARD'S SCROLL AND ODLAW'S BINOCULARS.

THERE ARE ALSO 25 WALLY-WATCHERS, EACH OF WHOM APPEARS ONLY ONCE SOMEWHERE ON MY TRAVELS. AND ONE MORE THING! CAN YOU FIND ANOTHER CHARACTER, NOT SHOWN BELOW, WHO APPEARS ONCE IN EVERY PICTURE?

Wally

THE GREAT WHERE'S WALLY NOW? CHECKLIST: PART ONE

Hundreds more things for time travellers to look for! Don't forget PART TWO at the end of this adventure!

THE STONE AGE

- [ ] Four cavemen swinging into trouble
- [ ] An accident with an axe
- [ ] A great invention
- [ ] A Stone-Age rodeo
- [ ] Boars chasing a man
- [ ] Men chasing a boar
- [ ] A romantic caveman
- [ ] A mammoth squirt
- [ ] A man who has overeaten
- [ ] A bear trap
- [ ] A mammoth in the river
- [ ] A fruit stall
- [ ] Charging woolly rhinos
- [ ] A big cover-up
- [ ] A trunk holding a trunk
- [ ] A knock-out game of baseball
- [ ] A rocky picture show
- [ ] An upside-down boar
- [ ] A spoiled dog
- [ ] A lesson on dinosaurs
- [ ] A very scruffy family
- [ ] Some dangerous spear fishermen

THE RIDDLE OF THE PYRAMIDS

- [ ] An upside-down pyramid
- [ ] An upside-down sarcophagus
- [ ] A group of posing gods
- [ ] Two protruding hands
- [ ] Two protruding feet
- [ ] A fat man and his picture
- [ ] Seventeen protruding tongues
- [ ] Stones defying gravity
- [ ] Egyptian vandals
- [ ] Egyptian graffiti
- [ ] A man sweeping dirt under a pyramid
- [ ] A thirsty sphinx
- [ ] A runaway block of stone
- [ ] Two weedy builders
- [ ] A cheeky builder
- [ ] A picture firing an arrow
- [ ] A careless water carrier
- [ ] Sunbathers in peril
- [ ] A messy milking session
- [ ] A mummy and a baby
- [ ] Pyramids of sand

FUN AND GAMES IN ANCIENT ROME

- [ ] A charioteer who has lost his chariot
- [ ] Coliseum cleaners
- [ ] An unequal contest with spears
- [ ] A winner who is about to lose
- [ ] A lion with good table manners
- [ ] A deadly set of wheels
- [ ] Lion cubs being teased
- [ ] Four shields that match their owners
- [ ] A pyramid of lions
- [ ] Lions giving the paws down
- [ ] A leopard chasing a leopard skin
- [ ] A piggyback puncher
- [ ] An awful musician
- [ ] A painful fork-lift
- [ ] A horse holding the reins
- [ ] A leopard in love
- [ ] A Roman keeping count
- [ ] A gladiator losing his sandals

ON TOUR WITH THE VIKINGS

- [ ] A happy figurehead
- [ ] Figureheads in love
- [ ] A man being used as a club
- [ ] A tearful sheep
- [ ] Two hopeless hiding places
- [ ] Childish Vikings
- [ ] A beard with a foot on it
- [ ] An eagle posing as a helmet
- [ ] A sailor tearing a sail
- [ ] A heavily armed Viking
- [ ] A patchy couple
- [ ] Three spears being beheaded
- [ ] A burning behind
- [ ] A bent boat
- [ ] A frightened figurehead
- [ ] Locked horns
- [ ] A helmet of spiders
- [ ] A helmet of smoke
- [ ] A bullfight

THE END OF THE CRUSADES

- [ ] A cat about to be catapulted
- [ ] A man about to be catapulted
- [ ] A human bridge
- [ ] A key that is out of reach
- [ ] A message for the milkman
- [ ] A cauldron of boiling oil
- [ ] A battering-ram
- [ ] Crusaders caught by their necks
- [ ] A load of washing
- [ ] Two catapult catastrophes
- [ ] A catapult aiming the wrong way
- [ ] Three snakes
- [ ] A crusader fast asleep
- [ ] Crusaders soaking up the sun
- [ ] Flattened crusaders
- [ ] Rockfaces
- [ ] A crusader who broke a ladder
- [ ] A ticklish situation

ONCE UPON A SATURDAY MORNING

- [ ] A dirty downpour
- [ ] Archers missing the target
- [ ] A jouster sitting back to front
- [ ] A dog stalking a cat stalking some birds
- [ ] A long line of pickpockets
- [ ] A jouster who needs lots of practice
- [ ] A man making a bear dance
- [ ] A bear making a man dance
- [ ] Hats that are tied together
- [ ] Fruit and vegetable thieves
- [ ] An unexpected puddle
- [ ] A juggling jester
- [ ] A very long drink
- [ ] A heavily burdened beast
- [ ] Drunken friars
- [ ] A man scything hats
- [ ] An angry fish
- [ ] A ticklish torture
- [ ] Minstrels making an awful noise

THE ABSOLUTELY HUGE AND ENORMOUSLY INTERESTING BOOK OF CAVEMEN, CAVE WOMEN, CAVE DOGS, AND ALL SORTS OF EXTREMELY SAVAGE STONE-AGE BEASTS.

HI THERE, BOOK WORMS!

SOME BITS OF HISTORY ARE AMAZING! I SIT HERE READING ALL THESE BOOKS ABOUT THE WORLD LONG AGO, AND IT'S LIKE RIDING A TIME MACHINE. WHY NOT TRY IT FOR YOURSELVES? JUST SEARCH EACH PICTURE AND FIND ME, WOOF (REMEMBER, ALL YOU CAN SEE IS HIS TAIL), WENDA, WIZARD WHITEBEARD AND ODLAW. THEN LOOK FOR MY KEY, WOOF'S BONE (IN THIS SCENE IT'S THE BONE THAT'S NEAREST TO HIS TAIL), WENDA'S CAMERA, WIZARD WHITEBEARD'S SCROLL AND ODLAW'S BINOCULARS.

THERE ARE ALSO 25 WALLY-WATCHERS, EACH OF WHOM APPEARS ONLY ONCE SOMEWHERE ON MY TRAVELS. AND ONE MORE THING! CAN YOU FIND ANOTHER CHARACTER, NOT SHOWN BELOW, WHO APPEARS ONCE IN EVERY PICTURE?

Wally

4,578 YEARS AGO

THE RIDDLE OF THE PYRAMIDS

THE ANCIENT EGYPTIANS WERE VERY CLEVER PEOPLE WHO LOVED GOATS, CATS AND SPHINX, AND INVENTED PYRAMIDS. WITH GREAT DIFFICULTY THEY BUILT SEVERAL HUGE PYRAMIDS IN THE DESERT.

BUT NOW NO ONE CAN REMEMBER WHY. WERE THEY ADVENTURE PLAY-GROUNDS FOR EGYPTIAN MUMMIES AND BABIES, OR WERE THEY HOUSES WITHOUT ANY OF THE USE-FUL BITS? IS IT POSSIBLE (OR EVEN LIKELY) THAT PHARAOHS WERE BURIED UNDER THEM? THESE QUESTIONS ARE AS HARD TO ANSWER AS A CAMEL'S HUMP.

2,000 YEARS AGO

FVN AND GAMES IN ANCIENT ROME

THE ROMANS SPENT MOST OF THEIR TIME FIGHTING, CONQVERING, LEARNING LATIN AND MAKING ROADS. WHEN THEY TOOK THEIR HOLIDAYS, THEY ALWAYS HAD GAMES AT THE COLISEVM (AN OLD SORT OF PLAYGROVND).

THEIR FAVOVRITE GAMES WERE FIGHTING, MORE FIGHTING, CHARIOT RACING, FIGHTING AND FEEDING CHRISTIANS TO LIONS. WHEN THE CROWD GAVE A GLADIATOR THE THVMBS DOWN, IT MEANT KILL YOVR OPPONENT. THVMBS VP MEANT LET HIM GO, TO FIGHT TO THE DEATH ANOTHER DAY.

1,003 YEARS AGO

ON TOUR WITH THE VIKINGS

At home the Vikings were quiet people, who liked knitting and cheese tasting and boring things like that. But on tour they went wild. They put on their best horned hats and sailed across the sea, singing and shouting like mad. If you heard them coming, it was best to run away; because once they had arrived and unpacked their axes, there was no holding them back.

800 YEARS AGO

The End of the Crusades

After 200 years of fierce argument with the Saladins and Paladins, who would not tell them the way to Jerusalem, the Crusaders finally ran out of clean tee-shirts, so they came home. For years afterwards they dined out on stories of the lovely castles they had battered and besieged and the fascinating people they had thrown rocks at, so the Crusades were not a complete waste of time after all.

600 YEARS AGO

ONCE UPON A SATURDAY MORNING

The Middle Ages were a very merry time to be alive, especially on Saturdays, as long as you didn't get caught. Short skirts and stripy tights were in fashion for men; everybody knew lots of jokes; there was widespread juggling and jousting and archery and jesting and fun. But if you got into trouble, the Middle Ages could be miserable. For the man in the stocks or the pillory or about to lose his head, Saturday morning was no laughing matter.

THE LAST DAYS OF THE AZTECS

The Aztecs lived in sunny Mexico and were rich and strong and liked swinging from poles pretending to be eagles. They also liked making human sacrifices to their gods, so it was best to agree with everything they said. The Spanish were also rich and strong, and some of them, called conquistadors, came to Mexico in 1519 to have an adventure. They thought the Aztecs were a complete nuisance, only good for arguing with and fighting.

400 YEARS AGO

Is red better than blue? What do you mean, your poem about cherry blossom is better than mine? Shall we have another cup of tea? Over difficult questions such as these, the Japanese fought fiercely for hundreds of years. The fiercest fighters of all were the samurai, who wore flags on their backs so that their mummies could find them. The fighters without flags were called ashigaru. They couldn't take a joke any better than the samurai, especially about their hair.

TROUBLE IN OLD JAPAN

250 YEARS AGO

BEING A PIRATE
(Shiver-me-timbers!)

It was really a lot of fun being a pirate, especially if you were very hairy and didn't have much in the way of brains. It also helped if you only had one leg, or one eye, or two noses, and had a pirate's hat with your name-tag sewn inside and a treasure-map and a rusty cutlass. Once there were lots of pirates, but they died out in the end because too many of them were men (which is not a good idea).

HAVING A BALL IN GAYE PAREE

The history of France has some very bad bits, like getting your head chopped off by Madame Guillotine in the French Revolution; and some very good bits, like the invention of smelly cheese. In 1870 Napoleon (the third one) threw a marvellous ball in Paris to celebrate 1870 being a good bit. All the beautiful people came and danced the night away to a band called the Third Republic.

THE GOLD RUSH

At the end of the 19th century large numbers of excited AMERICANS were fre-quently to be seen RUSHING headlong towards HOLES in the ground, hoping to find GOLD. Most of them never even found the holes in the ground. But at least they all had a GOOD DAY, with plenty of EXERCISE and FRESH AIR, which kept them HEALTHY. And health is much more valuable than GOLD . . . well, nearly more valuable . . . isn't it?

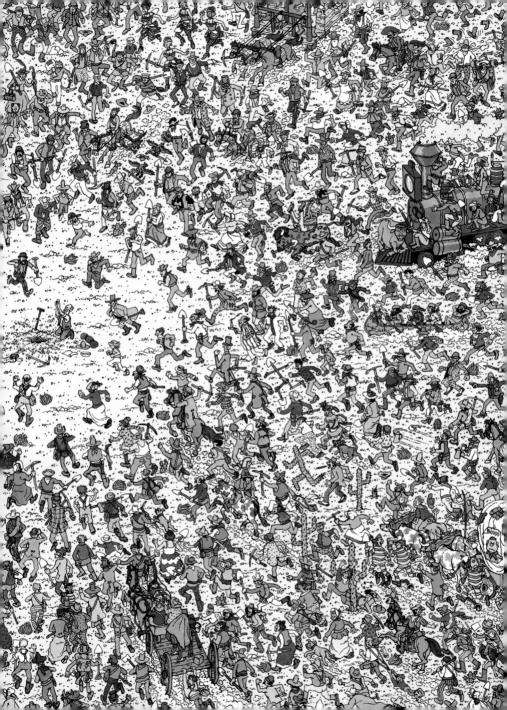

THE GREAT WHERE'S WALLY NOW?
CHECKLIST: PART TWO

THE GOLD RUSH

- An overloaded donkey
- A running cactus
- A man being dragged by his horse
- Running boots
- Running tools
- A man falling over a barrel
- A dog taking his pick
- A man on a buffalo
- A canoe out of water
- A clown on a unicycle
- Men who have come off the rails
- Prospecting vultures
- Three escaped convicts
- A man running into a cactus
- A moving house
- A man on a penny farthing
- Men in their night clothes
- A man being dragged by his dog
- Prospecting snakes
- A man taking a photograph
- A horse wearing a hat

BEING A PIRATE

- An unpopular woman
- A big pushover
- A pirate pinched by a crab
- A sniper in a palm tree
- A backfiring blunderbuss
- A pirate with four pistols and a sword
- Sharks ready to eat
- A skull with an eye patch
- A feeble cannon shot
- Feet sticking out of a cannon
- A modest figurehead
- A three-way clubbing
- A winking skull
- A creature with eight arms
- A crow's nest
- A cannonball puncher
- A deadly handshake
- A boat in a bathtub
- An empty treasure chest
- A cargo of heavyweights
- A human surfboard

THE LAST DAYS OF THE AZTECS

- A tall headdress
- Aztecs in a spin
- A conquistador with his fingers in his ears
- Three archers causing one man pain
- A picture looking sideways
- A tussle for a flag
- A human missile
- A drummer perched on high
- A kissing conquistador
- A frightened horse
- Yellow teeth
- A scabbard in the eye
- An eagle bombing raid
- A boy robbing a robber
- An Aztec ball game
- Five knock-outs with one slingshot

HAVING A BALL IN GAYE PAREE

- Can-can dancers
- Two musicians fighting with their bows
- A scruffy man
- A waiter spilling drink
- A man in a dress
- A tall thin man with a short fat woman
- A man caught by a statue
- Guests swinging from the chandeliers
- An eye-catching violinist
- A heavy pair of trousers
- A man about to get a crashing headache
- A man weighed down by his medals
- A curious assortment of weapons
- A man wearing a pile of hats
- An insolent statue
- A dangerous dancer
- A harpist firing an arrow
- A woman losing her dress

THE FUTURE

- A smiling satellite
- Mercury
- Hitch-hikers in the Galaxy
- Spaceships on a collision course
- A robot and his dog
- A creature holding six drinks
- Humans laughing at aliens
- A biplane
- Saturn being sat on
- Identical twin aliens
- Space traffic-lights
- An alien with two noses on his face
- Aliens laughing at humans
- A crash landing
- The Great Bear
- Costumes from every page of this book
- Flying saucers
- Neptune
- The Milky Way
- A blue alien with hand in pocket

TROUBLE IN OLD JAPAN

- Three warriors trapped on a bridge
- Warriors with daggers in their mouths
- A warrior caught by his pony-tail
- A sword being cut in two
- A warrior bending over backwards
- A wrestler out for the count
- An easily scared horse
- Warriors making a splash
- Warriors running under a bridge
- A heavy passenger
- A downtrodden warrior
- Two gangs of arrow thieves
- A shot under a hat
- A flag full of arrows
- A spear thrown backward

WHAT A MYSTERY!

Wow, Wally-watchers! As well as finding Wally and his friends, did you find all the things they lost? Did you find the mystery character in every picture? It may be difficult, but keep searching and eventually you'll find her (now, that's a clue!). And one last thing: somewhere one of the Wally-watchers lost the bobble from his hat. Can you spot which one and find the bobble?

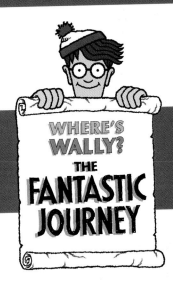

WHERE'S
WALLY?
THE
FANTASTIC
JOURNEY

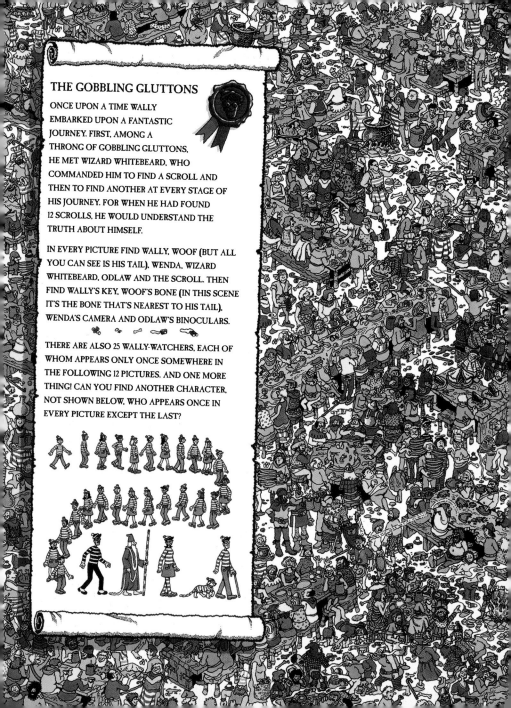

THE GOBBLING GLUTTONS

ONCE UPON A TIME WALLY
EMBARKED UPON A FANTASTIC
JOURNEY. FIRST, AMONG A
THRONG OF GOBBLING GLUTTONS,
HE MET WIZARD WHITEBEARD, WHO
COMMANDED HIM TO FIND A SCROLL AND
THEN TO FIND ANOTHER AT EVERY STAGE OF
HIS JOURNEY. FOR WHEN HE HAD FOUND
12 SCROLLS, HE WOULD UNDERSTAND THE
TRUTH ABOUT HIMSELF.

IN EVERY PICTURE FIND WALLY, WOOF (BUT ALL
YOU CAN SEE IS HIS TAIL), WENDA, WIZARD
WHITEBEARD, ODLAW AND THE SCROLL. THEN
FIND WALLY'S KEY, WOOF'S BONE (IN THIS SCENE
IT'S THE BONE THAT'S NEAREST TO HIS TAIL),
WENDA'S CAMERA AND ODLAW'S BINOCULARS.

THERE ARE ALSO 25 WALLY-WATCHERS, EACH OF
WHOM APPEARS ONLY ONCE SOMEWHERE IN
THE FOLLOWING 12 PICTURES. AND ONE MORE
THING! CAN YOU FIND ANOTHER CHARACTER,
NOT SHOWN BELOW, WHO APPEARS ONCE IN
EVERY PICTURE EXCEPT THE LAST?

THE GREAT WHERE'S WALLY? THE FANTASTIC JOURNEY CHECKLIST: PART ONE

Hundreds more things for Wally followers to look for! Don't forget PART TWO at the end of this adventure!

THE GOBBLING GLUTTONS

- A strong waiter and a weak one
- Long-distance smells
- Unequal portions of pie
- A man who has had too much to drink
- People who are going the wrong way
- Very tough dishes
- An upside-down dish
- A very hot dinner
- Knights drinking through straws
- A clever drink-pourer
- Giant sausages
- A custard fight
- An overloaded seat
- Beard-flavored soup
- Men pulling legs
- A painful spillage
- A poke in the eye
- A man tied up in spaghetti
- A knock-out dish
- A man who has eaten too much
- A tall diner eating a tall dish
- An exploding pie
- A giant sausage breaking in half
- A smell travelling through two people

THE BATTLING MONKS

- Two fire engines
- Hot-footed monks
- A bridge made of monks
- A cheeky monk
- A diving monk
- A scared statue
- Fire meeting water
- A snaking jet of water
- Chasers being chased
- A smug statue
- A snaking jet of flame
- A five-way wash-out
- A burning bridge
- Seven burning backsides
- Monks worshipping the Flowing Bucket of Water
- Monks shielding themselves from lava
- Thirteen trapped and extremely worried monks
- A monk seeing an oncoming jet of flame
- Monks worshipping the Mighty Erupting Volcano
- A very worried monk confronted by two opponents
- A burning hose
- Monks and lava pouring out of a volcano
- A chain of water
- Two monks accidentally attacking their brothers

THE CARPET FLYERS

- Two carpets on collison course
- An overweight flyer
- A pedestrian crossing
- A carpet pin-up
- Three hangers-on
- Flying hitch-hikers
- An unsatisfied customer
- A used carpet salesman
- A topsy-turvy tower
- A spiky crash
- Carpet cops and robbers
- A passing fruit thief
- Upside-down flyers
- A carpet repair shop
- Popular male and female flyers
- A flying tower
- A stair carpet
- Flying highwaymen
- Rich and poor flyers
- A carpet-breakdown rescue service
- Carpets flying on carpet flyers
- A carpet traffic policeman
- A flying carpet without a flyer

THE GREAT BALL-GAME PLAYERS

- A three-way drink
- A row of hand-held banners
- A chase that goes round in circles
- A spectator surrounded by three rival supporters
- Players who can't see where they are going
- Two tall players versus short ones
- Seven awful singers
- A face made of balls
- Players who are digging for victory
- A face about to hit a fist
- A shot that breaks the woodwork
- A mob chasing a player backwards
- A player chasing a mob
- Players pulling one another's hoods
- A flag with a hole in it
- A mob of players all holding balls
- A player heading a ball
- A player tripping over a rock
- A player punching a ball
- A spectator accidentally hitting two others
- A player poking his tongue out at a mob
- A mouth pulled open by a beard
- A backside shot

THE FEROCIOUS RED DWARFS

- A spear-breaking slingshot
- Two punches causing chain reactions
- Fat and thin spears and spearmen
- A spearman being knocked through a flag
- A collar made out of a shield
- A prison made of spears
- Tangled spears
- A devious disarmer
- Dwarfs disguised as spearmen
- A stick-up machine
- A spearman trapped by his battle dress
- A sneaky spear-bender
- An axe head causing headaches
- A dwarf who is on the wrong side
- Prankish target practice
- Opponents charging through each other
- A spearman running away from a spear
- A slingshot causing a chain reaction
- A sword cutting through a shield
- A dwarf hiding up a spear
- Spearmen who have jumped out of their clothes
- A spear knocking off a dwarf's helmet

THE NASTY NASTIES

- A vampire who is scared of ghosts
- Two vampire bears
- Vampires drinking through straws
- Gargoyle lovers
- An upside-down torture
- A baseball bat
- Three wolfmen
- A mummy who is coming undone
- A vampire mirror test
- A frightened skeleton
- Dog, cat and mouse doorways
- Courting cats
- A ghoulish game of skittles
- A gargoyle being poked in the eye
- An upside-down gargoyle
- Ghoulish flight controllers
- Three witches flying backwards
- A witch losing her broomstick
- A broomstick flying a witch
- A ticklish torture
- A vampire about to get the chop
- A ghost train
- A vampire who doesn't fit his coffin
- A three-eyed, hooded torturer

THE GOBBLING GLUTTONS

ONCE UPON A TIME WALLY
EMBARKED UPON A FANTASTIC
JOURNEY. FIRST, AMONG A
THRONG OF GOBBLING GLUTTONS,
HE MET WIZARD WHITEBEARD, WHO
COMMANDED HIM TO FIND A SCROLL AND
THEN TO FIND ANOTHER AT EVERY STAGE OF
HIS JOURNEY. FOR WHEN HE HAD FOUND
12 SCROLLS, HE WOULD UNDERSTAND THE
TRUTH ABOUT HIMSELF.

IN EVERY PICTURE FIND WALLY, WOOF (BUT ALL
YOU CAN SEE IS HIS TAIL), WENDA, WIZARD
WHITEBEARD, ODLAW AND THE SCROLL. THEN
FIND WALLY'S KEY, WOOF'S BONE (IN THIS SCENE
IT'S THE BONE THAT'S NEAREST TO HIS TAIL),
WENDA'S CAMERA AND ODLAW'S BINOCULARS.

THERE ARE ALSO 25 WALLY-WATCHERS, EACH OF
WHOM APPEARS ONLY ONCE SOMEWHERE IN
THE FOLLOWING 12 PICTURES. AND ONE MORE
THING! CAN YOU FIND ANOTHER CHARACTER,
NOT SHOWN BELOW, WHO APPEARS ONCE IN
EVERY PICTURE EXCEPT THE LAST?

THE BATTLING MONKS

THEN WALLY AND WIZARD WHITEBEARD CAME
TO THE PLACE WHERE THE INVISIBLE MONKS
OF FIRE FOUGHT THE MONKS OF WATER. AND
AS WALLY SEARCHED FOR THE SECOND SCROLL,
HE SAW THAT MANY WALLIES HAD BEEN THIS WAY BEFORE.
AND WHEN HE FOUND THE SCROLL, IT WAS TIME TO
CONTINUE WITH HIS JOURNEY.

THE CARPET FLYERS

THEN WALLY AND WIZARD WHITEBEARD CAME
TO THE LAND OF THE CARPET FLYERS, WHERE
MANY WALLIES HAD BEEN BEFORE. AND
WALLY SAW THAT THERE WERE MANY
CARPETS IN THE SKY AND MANY RED BIRDS
(HOW MANY, OH BRAINY BIRD AND CARPET WATCHERS?).
AND WHEN WALLY FOUND THE THIRD SCROLL, IT WAS
TIME TO CONTINUE WITH HIS JOURNEY.

THE GREAT BALL-GAME PLAYERS

THEN WALLY AND WIZARD WHITEBEARD CAME TO THE PLAYING FIELD OF THE GREAT BALL-GAME PLAYERS, WHERE MANY WALLIES HAD BEEN BEFORE. AND WALLY SAW THAT FOUR TEAMS WERE PLAYING AGAINST EACH OTHER (BUT WAS ANYONE WINNING? WHAT WAS THE SCORE? CAN YOU WORK OUT THE RULES?). THEN WALLY FOUND THE FOURTH SCROLL AND CONTINUED WITH HIS JOURNEY.

THE FEROCIOUS RED DWARVES

THEN WALLY AND WIZARD WHITEBEARD CAME
AMONG THE FEROCIOUS RED DWARVES, WHERE
MANY WALLIES HAD BEEN BEFORE. AND THE
DWARVES WERE ATTACKING THE MANY-COLOURED
SPEARMEN, CAUSING MIGHTY MAYHEM AND HORRID
HAVOC. AND WALLY FOUND THE FIFTH SCROLL, AND
CONTINUED WITH HIS JOURNEY.

THE NASTY NASTIES

THEN WALLY AND WIZARD WHITEBEARD CAME TO
THE CASTLE OF THE NASTY NASTIES, WHERE
MANY WALLIES HAD BEEN BEFORE. AND
WHEREVER WALLY WALKED, THERE WAS A CLATTERING
OF BONES (WOOF'S BONE IN THIS SCENE IS THE NEAREST TO
HIS TAIL) AND A FOUL SLURPING OF FILTHY FOOD. AND WALLY
FOUND THE SIXTH SCROLL AND CONTINUED WITH HIS JOURNEY.

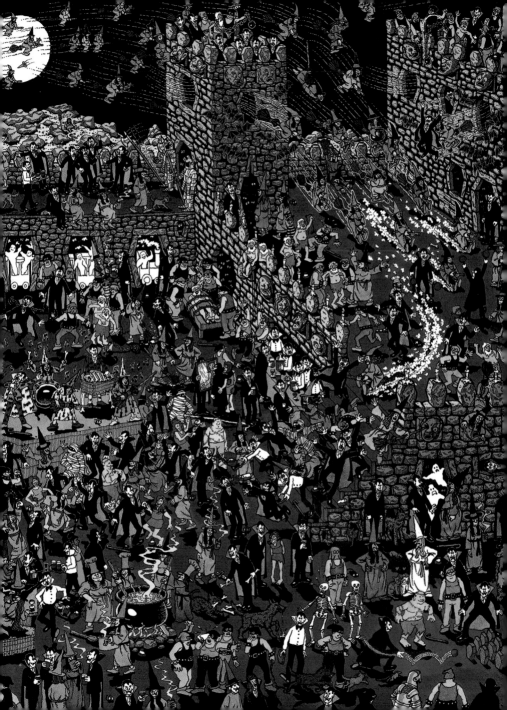

THE FIGHTING FORESTERS

THEN WALLY AND WIZARD WHITEBEARD CAME
AMONG THE FIGHTING FORESTERS, WHERE
MANY WALLIES HAD BEEN BEFORE. AND IN THEIR
BATTLE WITH THE EVIL BLACK KNIGHTS, THE
FOREST WOMEN WERE AIDED BY THE ANIMALS, BY THE LIVING
MUD, EVEN BY THE TREES THEMSELVES. AND WALLY FOUND THE
SEVENTH SCROLL AND CONTINUED WITH HIS JOURNEY.

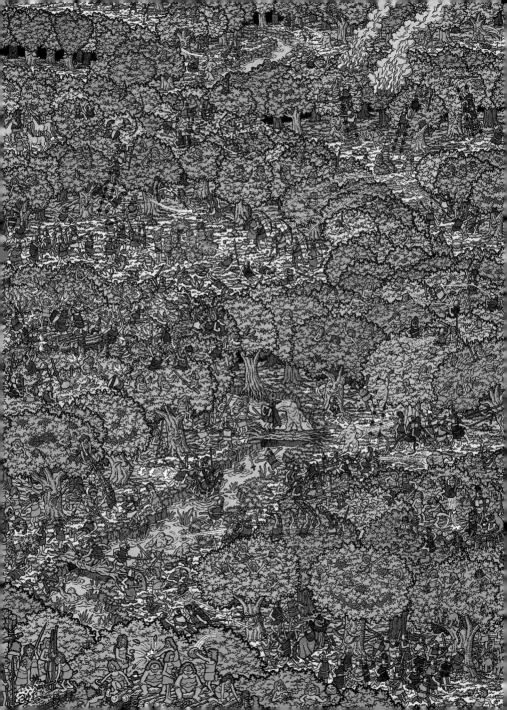

THE DEEP-SEA DIVERS

THEN WALLY AND WIZARD WHITEBEARD CAME TO
THE WATERY WORLD OF THE DEEP-SEA DIVERS,
WHERE MANY WALLIES HAD BEEN BEFORE. AND
WALLY SEARCHED FOR THE EIGHTH SCROLL AMONG
THE MONSTERS OF THE DEEP, AMONG THE MERMAIDS,
FISHERMEN AND FISH. AND WHEN HE FOUND IT, IT WAS TIME
TO CONTINUE WITH HIS JOURNEY.

THE KNIGHTS OF THE MAGIC FLAG

THEN WALLY AND WIZARD WHITEBEARD CAME
TO A PLACE MORE CROWDED THAN ANY WALLY
HAD SEEN BEFORE, WHERE TWO ARMIES WITH
MANY MAGIC FLAGS WERE LOCKED IN COMBAT.
AND WALLY SAW THAT MANY WALLIES HAD BEEN THIS WAY
BEFORE. AND WHEN HE FOUND THE NINTH SCROLL, IT WAS
TIME TO CONTINUE WITH HIS JOURNEY.

THE UNFRIENDLY GIANTS

THEN WALLY AND WIZARD WHITEBEARD CAME TO THE LAND OF THE UNFRIENDLY GIANTS, WHERE MANY WALLIES HAD BEEN BEFORE, AND WALLY SAW THAT THE GIANTS WERE HORRIDLY HARASSING THE LITTLE PEOPLE, AND WHEN HE FOUND THE TENTH SCROLL, IT WAS TIME TO CONTINUE WITH HIS JOURNEY.

THE UNDERGROUND HUNTERS

THEN WALLY AND WIZARD WHITEBEARD CAME
AMONG THE UNDERGROUND HUNTERS, WHERE
MANY WALLIES HAD BEEN BEFORE. AND THERE
WAS MUCH MENACE IN THIS PLACE, AND A
MULTITUDE OF MALEVOLENT MONSTERS. AND
WALLY FOUND THE ELEVENTH SCROLL AND CONTINUED
WITH HIS JOURNEY.

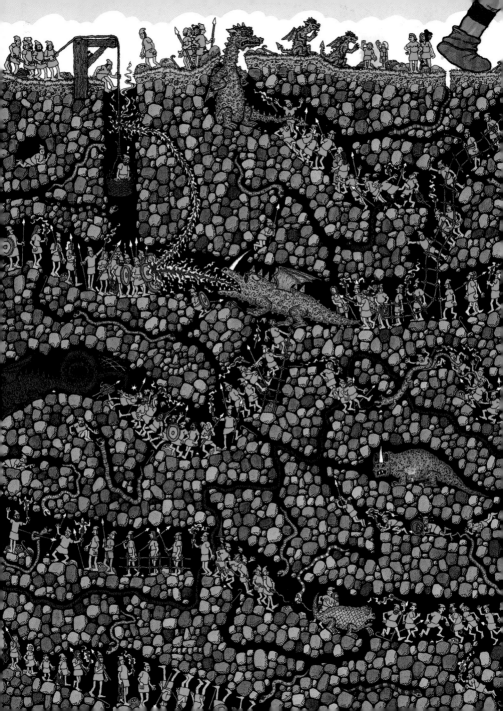

THE LAND OF WALLIES

THEN WALLY FOUND THE TWELFTH SCROLL AND SAW THE
TRUTH ABOUT HIMSELF, THAT HE WAS JUST ONE WALLY
AMONG MANY. HE SAW TOO THAT WALLIES OFTEN LOSE
THINGS. FOR HE HIMSELF HAD LOST ONE SHOE. AND AS
HE LOOKED FOR HIS SHOE, HE DISCOVERED THAT WIZARD
WHITEBEARD WAS NOT HIS ONLY FELLOW TRAVELLER. THERE WERE NOW
ELEVEN OTHERS - ONE FROM EVERY PLACE HE HAD BEEN TO -
WHO HAD JOINED HIM ONE BY ONE ALONG THE WAY. SO NOW (OH LOYAL
FOLLOWERS OF WALLY!) FIND THE REAL WALLY AND HELP HIM FIND HIS
MISSING SHOE. AND THERE, IN THE LAND OF WALLIES,
MAY WALLY LIVE HAPPILY EVER AFTER.

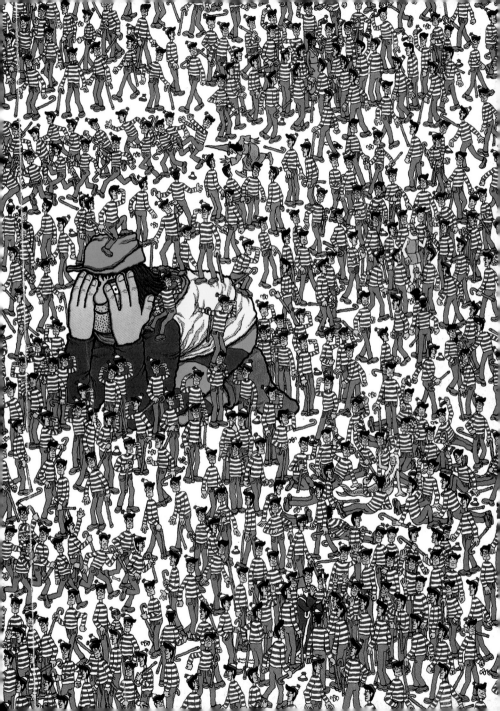

THE GREAT WHERE'S WALLY?
THE FANTASTIC JOURNEY CHECKLIST: PART TWO

THE FIGHTING FORESTERS

- Three long legs
- A three-legged knight
- Knights being chopped down by a tree
- Two multiple knock-outs
- A lazy lady
- A tree with a lot of puff
- Hard-headed women
- Attackers about to be attacked
- A strong woman and a weak one
- An easily frightened horse
- Eight pairs of upside-down feet
- Knights shooting arrows at knights
- An upside-down ladder
- Loving trees
- An upside-down trunk
- A two-headed unicorn
- A unicorn in a tree
- Trees with two faces
- Muddy mud-slingers
- A tearful small tree
- Spears getting sharpened tips
- Trees branching out violently
- Stilts being chewed up

THE DEEP-SEA DIVERS

- A two-headed fish
- A sword fight with a swordfish
- A sea bed
- A fish face
- A catfish and a dogfish
- A jellyfish
- A fish with two tails
- A skate
- A sea lion
- Two fish-shaped formations
- Treacherous treasure
- Oyster-beds
- Tinned fish, flying fish and fish fingers
- Electric eels
- A deck of cards
- A bottle in a message
- A fake fin
- A back to front mermaid
- A seahorse–drawn carriage
- A boat's compass
- A fish catching men
- An underwater beach scene
- Divers drawing on an angry sea monster

THE KNIGHTS OF THE MAGIC FLAG

- Unfaithful royals
- A flag full of fists
- A game of noughts and crosses
- A sword-fighting reindeer
- A man behind bars
- A mouse among lions
- Flags within a flag
- A tangle of tongues
- A zebra crossing
- An eagle dropping an eyeful
- A puffing spoilsport
- A battering-ram door key
- Snakes and ladders
- A flame-throwing dragon
- Diminishing puddings
- A crown thief
- A thirsty lion
- A weapon's imbalance
- A foot being tickled by a feather
- Some cheeky soldiers
- A surrendering reindeer
- A dog straining to get a bone
- A helmet with three eyes

THE UNFRIENDLY GIANTS

- Trappers about to be trapped
- A catapulted missile hitting people
- A hairy bird's nest
- Ducks out of water
- A mocking giant about to come unstuck
- Two broom trees
- Two giants who are out for the count
- Two windmill knock-outs
- A polite giant about to get a headache
- A giant with a roof over his head
- Three people in a giant hood
- A battering-fist
- A house shaker
- A drawing pin trap
- A landslide of boulders
- Six people strapped inside giant belts
- People being swept off their feet
- People taking part in a board game
- Rope-pullers being pulled
- Birds being disturbed by a giant
- Two game-watchers slapping people
- Four shy ladies being flattered
- A powerful burst of pond water

THE UNDERGROUND HUNTERS

- A hunter about to put his foot in it
- Four frightened flames
- A snaky hat thief
- An underground traffic policeman
- Three surrendering flames
- A two-headed snake
- A snaky tickle
- A ridiculously long snake
- Three dragons wearing sunglasses
- A dragon that attacks with both ends
- Angry snake-parents
- Five broken spears
- A monstrous bridge
- Five rock faces
- Upside-down hunters
- A snake that is trapped
- A very long ladder
- A torch setting fire to spears
- Hunters tripped by a tongue
- A hunter with an extra long spear
- Hunters about to collide
- Hunters going round in a circle
- A shocked tail-puller

THE LAND OF WALLIES

- Wallies waving
- Wallies walking
- Wallies running
- Wallies sitting
- Wallies lying down
- Wallies sliding
- Wallies standing still
- Wallies smiling
- Wallies searching
- Wallies being chased
- Wallies giving the thumbs up
- Wallies looking frightened
- Wallies with bobble hats
- Wallies without bobble hats
- Wallies raising their bobble hats
- Wallies with walking sticks
- Wallies without walking sticks
- Wallies with spectacles
- Wallies without spectacles
- A Wally on a hat
- A Wally holding a wing
- Wally

THE FANTASTIC JOURNEY

Did you find Wally, his friends and all the things that they had lost? Did you find the mystery character who appeared in every scene except the Land of Wallies? It may be difficult, but keep searching and eventually you'll find him – now that's a clue! And one last thing: somewhere one of the Wally-watchers lost the bobble from his hat. Can you find which one, and find the bobble?

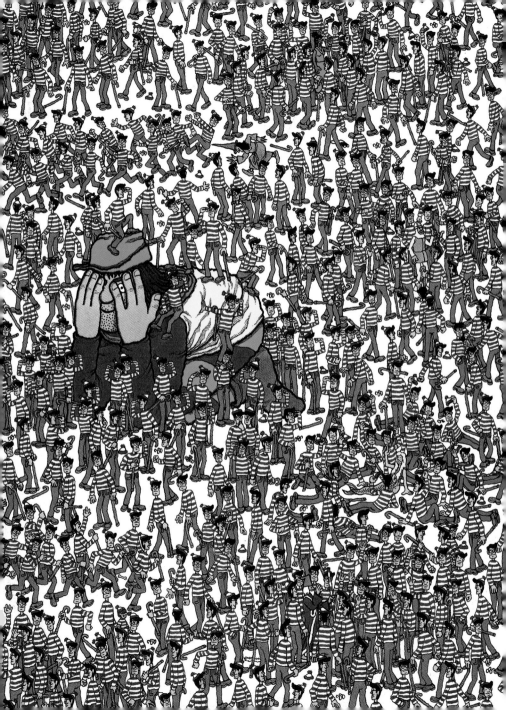

A DREAM COME TRUE

WOW, WALLY-WATCHERS, THIS IS FANTASTIC, I'M REALLY IN HOLLYWOOD! LOOK AT THE FILM PEOPLE EVERYWHERE – I WONDER WHAT MOVIES THEY'RE MAKING. THIS IS MY DREAM COME TRUE ... TO MEET THE DIRECTORS AND ACTORS, TO WALK THROUGH THE CROWDS OF EXTRAS, TO SEE BEHIND THE SCENES! PHEW, I WONDER IF I'LL APPEAR IN A MOVIE MYSELF!

★ ★ ★ WHAT TO LOOK FOR IN HOLLYWOOD! ★ ★ ★

WELCOME TO TINSELTOWN, WALLY-WATCHERS! THESE ARE THE PEOPLE AND THINGS TO LOOK FOR AS YOU WALK THROUGH THE FILM SETS WITH WALLY.

★ FIRST (OF COURSE!) WHERE'S WALLY?

★ NEXT FIND WALLY'S CANINE COMPANION, WOOF – REMEMBER, ALL YOU CAN SEE IS HIS TAIL!

★ THEN FIND WALLY'S FRIEND, WENDA!

★ ABRACADABRA! NOW FOCUS IN ON WIZARD WHITEBEARD!

★ BOO! HISS! HERE COMES THE BAD GUY, ODLAW!

★ NOW SPOT THESE 25 WALLY-WATCHERS, EACH OF WHOM APPEARS ONLY ONCE BEFORE THE FINAL FANTASTIC SCENE!

★ WOW! INCREDIBLE! SPOT ONE OTHER CHARACTER WHO APPEARS IN EVERY SCENE EXCEPT THE LAST!

★ ★ KEEP ON SEARCHING! THERE'S MORE TO FIND! ★ ★

ON EVERY SET FIND WALLY'S LOST KEY!
WOOF'S LOST BONE! WENDA'S LOST CAMERA! WIZARD WHITEBEARD'S SCROLL! ODLAW'S LOST BINOCULARS! AND A MISSING CAN OF FILM!

★ ★ ★ ★ ★ ★ AND MORE AND MORE! ★ ★ ★ ★ ★ ★ ★

EACH OF THE FOUR POSTERS ON THE WALL OVER THERE IS PART OF ONE OF THE FILM SETS WALLY IS ABOUT TO VISIT. ★ FIND OUT WHERE THE POSTERS CAME FROM. ★ THEN SPOT ANY DIFFERENCES BETWEEN THE POSTERS AND THE SETS.

THE GREAT WHERE'S WALLY? IN HOLLYWOOD CHECKLIST: PART ONE

Lots more things for Wally-watchers to look for! Don't forget PART TWO at the end of this adventure!

★ ★ ★ A DREAM COME TRUE ★ ★ ★

- [ ] A soldier capturing some food
- [ ] A double agent in a spy film
- [ ] Someone walking tall
- [ ] A swing band
- [ ] A green star on a yellow ball
- [ ] A wind machine blowing out of control
- [ ] A romantic scene
- [ ] A girl in a swimsuit with a yellow hat
- [ ] Eight pieces of heart-shaped film equipment
- [ ] Ten studio security guards
- [ ] Twenty-one pirates in striped clothing
- [ ] Three shields
- [ ] Someone who has put their foot in it
- [ ] Three people with skis
- [ ] A scenic painter
- [ ] A man with a red-and-white-spotted tie
- [ ] A friendly pirate

★ ★ SHHH! THIS IS A SILENT MOVIE ★ ★

- [ ] A watchtower
- [ ] Two mobile cameras
- [ ] A director with a giant loud hailer
- [ ] A searchlight
- [ ] A runaway wheel
- [ ] Two butterfly catchers
- [ ] Thirteen balloons
- [ ] A man in plus-four trousers
- [ ] Seven loud hailers
- [ ] A trail of leaking buckets
- [ ] Nine four-legged animals
- [ ] Fifteen cameras
- [ ] Some flowers being watered
- [ ] Three men tripping on some fruit
- [ ] A hose cut by an axe
- [ ] Four fire chiefs wearing pointed hats
- [ ] A railway-track ladder
- [ ] Three men wearing red shirts and braces
- [ ] Two umbrellas

★ ★ ★ HORSEPLAY IN TROY ★ ★ ★

- [ ] Five blue soldiers with red-crested helmets
- [ ] One soldier wearing sandals
- [ ] Thirteen real four-legged animals
- [ ] Some ancient traffic police
- [ ] Five red soldiers with blue-crested helmets
- [ ] Two soldiers with slings
- [ ] Four first-aid soldiers
- [ ] Five yellow soldiers with blue-crested helmets
- [ ] Five soldiers with brooms
- [ ] One soldier with a square shield
- [ ] Three film crew members wearing sunglasses
- [ ] Three soldiers with extra-long cloaks
- [ ] Two statues waving at each other
- [ ] Three Trojans drinking coffee
- [ ] Ten arrows that are stuck in shields
- [ ] A litter bin
- [ ] Soldiers arguing about the time

★ ★ FUN IN THE FOREIGN LEGION ★ ★

- [ ] Some date trees
- [ ] Twelve camels
- [ ] A modern aeroplane ruining a camera shot
- [ ] Four trees surrendering
- [ ] A rock hitting sixteen people
- [ ] Two men being shaken out of a tree
- [ ] The right costumes in the wrong colours
- [ ] A horseman riding in the wrong direction
- [ ] A French flag with colours in the wrong order
- [ ] Five men wearing vests and shorts
- [ ] Some enemies fighting back-to-back
- [ ] An unpopular musician
- [ ] A man reading a newspaper
- [ ] Three men hiding underneath animals
- [ ] An animal treading on a man's foot
- [ ] A man surrendering to a shovel

★ A TREMENDOUS SONG AND DANCE ★

- [ ] One dancer wearing a blue carnation
- [ ] Some tap dancers
- [ ] A grand piano
- [ ] A musician playing a double bass
- [ ] Dancers wearing top hat and tails
- [ ] Sailors saluting the ship's "N" sign
- [ ] The captain's log
- [ ] Sailors with bell-bottom pants
- [ ] A vice admiral
- [ ] A piano keyboard
- [ ] Four orange feathers
- [ ] A soldier on the wrong set
- [ ] Five real anchors
- [ ] Three watery creatures
- [ ] Nine mops
- [ ] Four sailors with tattoos

★ ALI BABA AND THE FORTY THIEVES ★

- [ ] A man asleep in bed
- [ ] Another man awake in bed
- [ ] Five animals
- [ ] A man wearing yellow shoes
- [ ] A man wearing green shoes
- [ ] A man wearing a red shoe and a white shoe
- [ ] A man wearing a red shoe and a pink shoe
- [ ] A chest of drawers
- [ ] A man with jewels in his beard
- [ ] Two careless carpet carriers
- [ ] A man wearing a green turban
- [ ] A man wearing a yellow turban
- [ ] Four real genies
- [ ] A man carrying a grey treasure chest
- [ ] A man with a red star on his turban
- [ ] A man with a yellow tassel on his fez
- [ ] A man with a green tassel on his fez

★ ★ ★ THE WILD, WILD WEST ★ ★ ★

- [ ] Two cowboys about to draw against each other
- [ ] Drinkers raising their glasses to a lady
- [ ] Outlaws holding up a stagecoach
- [ ] Some boisterous cowboys painting the town red
- [ ] Doc holiday
- [ ] The film wardrobe department
- [ ] Buffalo Bill
- [ ] The loan ranger
- [ ] Gamblers playing cards
- [ ] A couple of gunslingers
- [ ] Calamity Jane
- [ ] A buffalo **stamp**ede
- [ ] A spaghetti western
- [ ] A horse-drawn wagon
- [ ] Billy the kid
- [ ] Townspeople saluting General Store
- [ ] A band of outlaws
- [ ] Two cowboys shouting, "This town ain't big enough for the both of us."

A DREAM COME TRUE

WOW, WALLY-WATCHERS, THIS IS FANTASTIC, I'M REALLY IN HOLLYWOOD! LOOK AT THE FILM PEOPLE EVERYWHERE – I WONDER WHAT MOVIES THEY'RE MAKING. THIS IS MY DREAM COME TRUE ... TO MEET THE DIRECTORS AND ACTORS, TO WALK THROUGH THE CROWDS OF EXTRAS, TO SEE BEHIND THE SCENES! PHEW, I WONDER IF I'LL APPEAR IN A MOVIE MYSELF!

★ ★ ★ WHAT TO LOOK FOR IN HOLLYWOOD! ★ ★ ★

WELCOME TO TINSELTOWN, WALLY-WATCHERS! THESE ARE THE PEOPLE AND THINGS TO LOOK FOR AS YOU WALK THROUGH THE FILM SETS WITH WALLY.

* FIRST (OF COURSE!) WHERE'S WALLY?

* NEXT FIND WALLY'S CANINE COMPANION, WOOF – REMEMBER, ALL YOU CAN SEE IS HIS TAIL!

* THEN FIND WALLY'S FRIEND, WENDA!

* ABRACADABRA! NOW FOCUS IN ON WIZARD WHITEBEARD!

* BOO! HISS! HERE COMES THE BAD GUY, ODLAW!

* NOW SPOT THESE 25 WALLY-WATCHERS, EACH OF WHOM APPEARS ONLY ONCE BEFORE THE FINAL FANTASTIC SCENE!

* WOW! INCREDIBLE! SPOT ONE OTHER CHARACTER WHO APPEARS IN EVERY SCENE EXCEPT THE LAST!

★ ★ KEEP ON SEARCHING! THERE'S MORE TO FIND! ★ ★

ON EVERY SET FIND WALLY'S LOST KEY!
WOOF'S LOST BONE! WENDA'S LOST CAMERA! WIZARD WHITEBEARD'S SCROLL!
ODLAW'S LOST BINOCULARS! AND A MISSING CAN OF FILM!

★ ★ ★ ★ ★ ★ AND MORE AND MORE! ★ ★ ★ ★ ★ ★

EACH OF THE FOUR POSTERS ON THE WALL OVER THERE IS PART OF ONE OF THE FILM SETS WALLY IS ABOUT TO VISIT. * FIND OUT WHERE THE POSTERS CAME FROM. * THEN SPOT ANY DIFFERENCES BETWEEN THE POSTERS AND THE SETS.

SHHH! THIS IS A SILENT MOVIE

SO THIS IS HOW THE HOLLYWOOD DREAM BEGAN — WITH SILENT MOVIES MADE IN BLACK AND WHITE. IT LOOKS CRAZY AND IT MAKES YOU LAUGH. ACTING IN SLAPSTICK COMEDIES MUST BE REALLY HARD — LOOK HOW MANY ACCIDENTS ARE HAPPENING. BUT THE GREAT THING IS THAT NONE OF THE ACTORS EVER GET HURT, HOWEVER OFTEN THEY FALL FLAT ON THEIR FACES!

HORSEPLAY IN TROY

WHAT A SPECTACULAR SCENE THIS IS, WALLY-WATCHERS! AND WHAT AN EPIC COMMOTION PICTURE! I WONDER WHY THE TROJANS DIDN'T GUESS THE WOODEN HORSE WAS FULL OF GREEKS, AND HOW DID THEY GET IT THROUGH THE GATES OF TROY ANYWAY? I WOULDN'T LIKE TO BE IN THE TROJANS' SANDALS, IF THE COSTUME DEPARTMENT HAD GIVEN THEM ANY, THAT IS!

FUN IN THE FOREIGN LEGION

PHEW, FILM FANS, DON'T GET OVERHEATED, THIS IS
THE MOST SIZZLING LOCATION SO FAR! EVERYONE'S
SWELTERING, FROM STARS TO SAND-SHIFTERS. SOME
OF THOSE EXTRAS LOOK LIKE THEY'RE LOSING THEIR
COOL – HAVE THEY FORGOTTEN THIS IS ONLY A FILM?
PERHAPS IT'S TIME A FEW MORE OF THEM DESERTED
THE DESERT AND JOINED THE RUSH FOR ICE-CREAM!

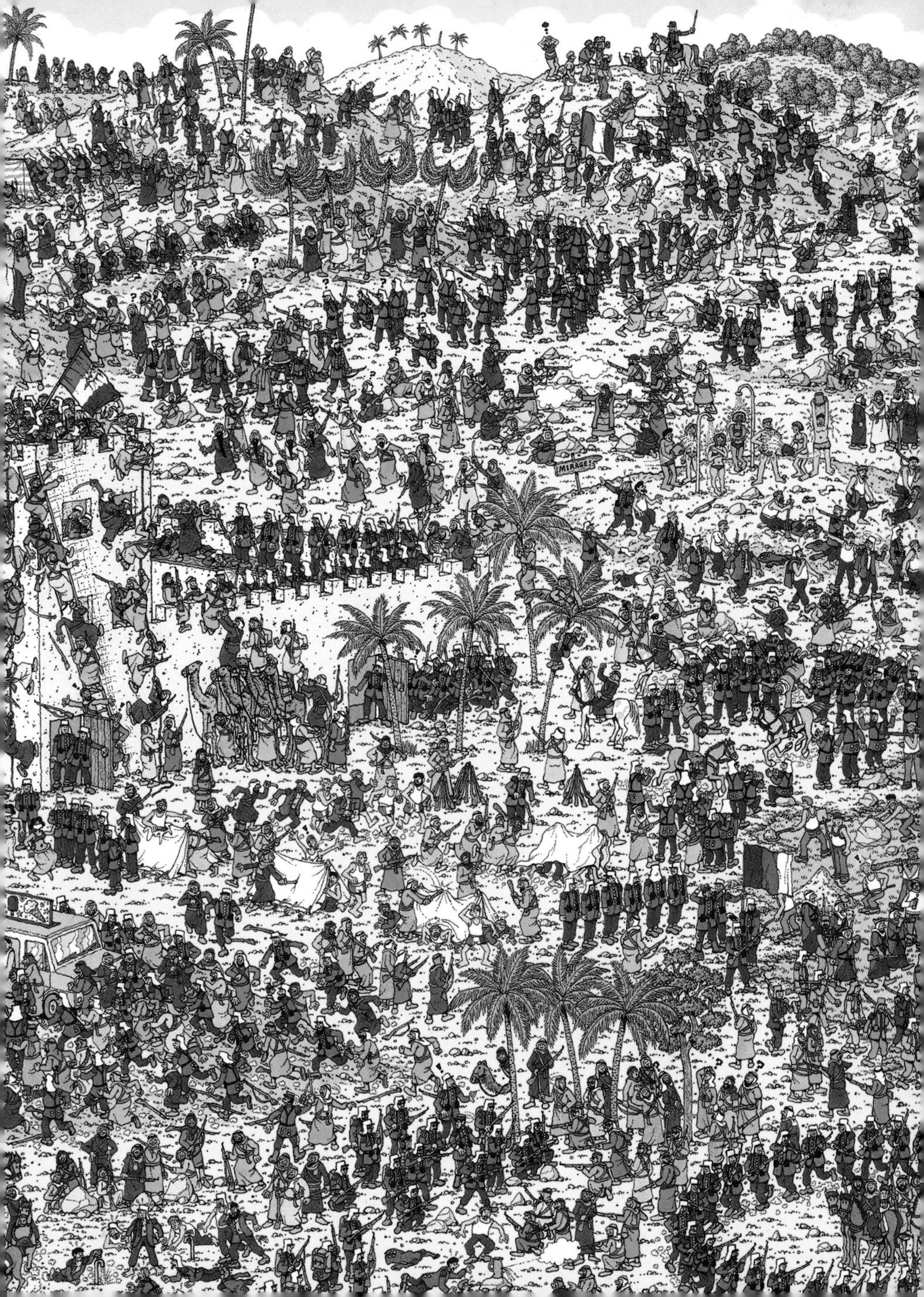
MIRAGE!

ALI BABA AND THE FORTY THIEVES

WHAT A CRUSH IN THE CAVE, WALLY-FOLLOWERS, BUT PAN IN ON THOSE POTS OF TREASURE! HOW MANY THIEVES WERE IN THE STORY? I BELIEVE THIS DIRECTOR THINKS FORTY THOUSAND! HAVE YOU SPOTTED ALI BABA? HE'S IN THE ALLEY, CUTTING HAIR – THE SCRIPTWRITER THINKS HIS NAME'S ALLEY BARBER! JANGLING GENIES – WHAT A FEARFULLY FUNNY FLICK THIS IS!

THE SWASHBUCKLING MUSKETEERS

ALL FOR ONE, ONE FOR ALL! — WASN'T THAT THE
MOTTO OF THE THREE MUSKETEERS? NOW LOOK
AT THIS FREE-FOR-ALL! CAN YOU SPOT OUR THREE
GALLANT HEROES BATTLING WITH THE RED-COATED
CARDINAL'S GUARDS? WITH ALL THIS SWASHBUCKLING
ACTION GOING ON, I WONDER HOW THE CAMERAMEN
CAN CAPTURE IT ALL ON FILM!

DINOSAURS, SPACEMEN AND GHOULS

PHEW, INCREDIBLE! TIME, SPACE AND HORROR ARE IN A MIGHTY MUDDLE HERE! WHAT COSMIC COSTUMES AND WHAT GREAT SPECIAL EFFECTS! ONE OF THOSE FLYING SAUCERS LOOKS LIKE IT'S REALLY FLYING! ARE THOSE REAL ALIENS INSIDE, NOT ACTORS AT ALL? SO WHAT'S REAL AND WHAT'S MADE UP IN FILMS LIKE THESE?

WHEN THE STARS COME OUT

WOW, WALLY-WATCHERS, THIS IS WHAT I CALL GLAMOUR! I'M AT A MAJOR MOVIE PREMIERE. THE STARS HAVE COME TO SEE THE FILM, THE CROWDS HAVE COME TO SEE THE STARS. LOOK AT THAT PINK STRETCH LIMO — NOW THAT'S A PROPER CAR FOR A STAR. AND WHO'S IN THE BONE-MOBILE BEHIND? AND DOESN'T KING KONG LOOK NICER IN LIFE THAN WHEN HE'S ON THE SCREEN?

WHERE'S WALLY? THE MUSICAL

WOW, WHAT AN EXTRAVAGANZA, WALLY-WATCHERS – THIS ALL-SINGING, ALL-DANCING MOVIE IS ALL ABOUT ME AND MY FRIENDS! LOOK HOW MANY ACTORS ARE DRESSED UP AS ME! AND LOOK AT ALL THE WOOFS, WENDAS, WIZARD WHITEBEARDS AND ODLAWS. HAVE YOU NOTICED THAT THE WARDROBE DEPARTMENT HAS MADE MISTAKES WITH SOME OF THE ACTORS' COSTUMES? BUT THAT WON'T HELP YOU FIND THE REAL ME AND MY FOUR FRIENDS IN THIS FILM! I'LL GIVE YOU SOME CLUES. I'M THE WALLY WITH SOMETHING EXTRA FOR WOOF. ALL YOU CAN SEE OF THE REAL WOOF IS HIS TAIL. THE REAL WENDA HAS A CAMERA. THE REAL WIZARD WHITEBEARD IS WEARING A HAT BENT TO THE LEFT. AND THE REAL ODLAW IS HOLDING A WALKING STICK.

THERE'S JUST ONE MORE THING. I'VE BEEN FOLLOWED HERE BY ONE CHARACTER FROM EVERY SET I'VE VISITED. SO CAN YOU SPOT ALL ELEVEN OF THEM IN THIS SCENE? AND CAN YOU FIND OUT WHEN EACH CHARACTER FIRST JOINED ME; AND CATCH ALL THEIR APPEARANCES THROUGHOUT MY TRAVELS?

THE GREAT WHERE'S WALLY? IN HOLLYWOOD CHECKLIST: PART TWO

Even more things for Wally-watchers to look for.

★ THE SWASHBUCKLING MUSKETEERS ★

- [ ] Eleven gentlemen bowing
- [ ] Two wheelbarrows
- [ ] Twelve spouts of water
- [ ] A tear-jerking emotional scene
- [ ] A gentleman with only one glove
- [ ] Three musket tears
- [ ] One lost glove
- [ ] A man wearing different coloured gloves
- [ ] A hat with a striped plume
- [ ] Badly dressed men turned away from the dance
- [ ] A bouncer
- [ ] Two swordfighting ladies
- [ ] Two duelling film directors
- [ ] Three angry gardeners
- [ ] Two swordsmen fencing
- [ ] Three mixed-up statues
- [ ] A man having his foot tickled
- [ ] Four ladies being presented with flowers
- [ ] Four real animals

★ DINOSAURS, SPACEMEN AND GHOULS ★

- [ ] "Hand" luggage
- [ ] A fly in saucer
- [ ] A ticklish dinosaur
- [ ] A greedy green alien
- [ ] A dozing dinosaur
- [ ] A spaceship
- [ ] A cheeky dinosaur
- [ ] Stars in a star's dressing room
- [ ] A wolfman having a howling good time
- [ ] Eight characters in craters
- [ ] A planet picnic
- [ ] A game of hoopla
- [ ] A spacecastle
- [ ] Two people reading books
- [ ] Four cavemen going up in the world
- [ ] An astronaut without helmet, gloves or boots
- [ ] Three other astronauts without helmets
- [ ] Two bottles of ketchup

★ ROBIN HOOD'S MERRY MESS-UP ★

- [ ] Eight ladies in medieval costume
- [ ] "Little" John leading some men
- [ ] Sixteen flags
- [ ] Two archers with long bows
- [ ] "Maid" Marian cleaning up
- [ ] A medieval extra with a radio
- [ ] A sheriff's soldier with rolled-up sleeves
- [ ] "Frier" Tuck
- [ ] A night in armour
- [ ] A knight with a pink plume in his helmet
- [ ] The Sheriff of Nottingham
- [ ] A man with a bow and arrow
- [ ] A soldier with a large shield
- [ ] Medieval soldiers wearing the wrong trousers
- [ ] A prisoner with a giant ball and chain
- [ ] Five real four-legged animals
- [ ] Twenty-one ladders
- [ ] Seven helmets with animal crests

★ ★ WHEN THE STARS COME OUT ★ ★

- [ ] Twenty-nine lights
- [ ] Two rival news reporters
- [ ] Someone who has it all wrapped up
- [ ] A policeman wanting an autograph
- [ ] Three cowboys
- [ ] Ten hearts
- [ ] Seven large palms
- [ ] Someone with a bird's-eye view
- [ ] A handful of spectators
- [ ] A celebrity wearing a new dress
- [ ] Someone making their mark
- [ ] Two astronauts
- [ ] A sleepy spectator with an alarm clock
- [ ] A twisting telescope
- [ ] An extra-long straw
- [ ] Four celebrities wearing sunglasses

★ ★ WHERE'S WALLY? THE MUSICAL ★ ★

- [ ] A Wally sweater with stripes in reverse order
- [ ] A Wally with blond hair
- [ ] A Wally with a beard
- [ ] A Wenda without any shoes
- [ ] A Wally wearing shades
- [ ] An Odlaw without a moustache
- [ ] A Wally jumper with extra stripes
- [ ] A haredresser
- [ ] A Wally wearing a hat without a bobble
- [ ] A Wally without pockets on his jeans
- [ ] A Wizard Whitebeard wearing glasses
- [ ] A Wally script reading
- [ ] A sound mixer
- [ ] A Wenda with a blue-and-white-striped umbrella
- [ ] A walking stick
- [ ] Two Wizard Whitebeards without beards
- [ ] A Wally without glasses
- [ ] An Odlaw wearing a hat without a bobble
- [ ] A Wenda with blonde hair
- [ ] A Wally wearing a bobble hat in reverse colours
- [ ] A Wenda without glasses
- [ ] A Wizard Whitebeard wearing a red hat
- [ ] A Woof wearing a bobble hat in reverse colours
- [ ] A Wenda wearing round Wally glasses
- [ ] A Wally tickling another Wally
- [ ] A Woof without a bobble hat
- [ ] A Wenda with no pockets on her skirt
- [ ] A Wally holding a walking stick the wrong way up
- [ ] A Woof wearing a hat without a bobble
- [ ] A Woof wearing shades
- [ ] A back view of a Wenda
- [ ] A Wally in blue and white stripes
- [ ] A Wenda who is not wearing a bobble hat
- [ ] An Odlaw without shades
- [ ] A Wizard Whitebeard dancing
- [ ] A back view of a Wally
- [ ] A Wizard Whitebeard wearing a bobble hat
- [ ] A Woof wearing a blue and white bobble hat
- [ ] Two Wizard Whitebeards without white beards
- [ ] A Wenda wearing a hat without a bobble
- [ ] A Wally with two bobble hats

★ ★ ★ BACK TO THE BEGINNING ★ ★ ★

Did you find Wally, all his friends and all the things they lost? Did you find the mystery character who appears in every scene except the last? And one more thing: somewhere one of the Wally-watchers lost the bobble from his hat. Can you spot which one and find the bobble?

★ ★ ★ THE FINAL FILM TEST ★ ★ ★

Nearly all the faces in the sprocket holes on this and on PART ONE of the checklist appear in colour somewhere else in the book. Can you find where? But . . . ten of them do not appear anywhere else! Can you tell which ten? Lastly . . . some faces appear more than once in the sprocket holes. Can you see which ones and how many times each one appears?

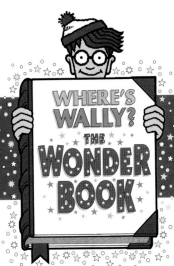

THE GREAT WHERE'S WALLY? THE WONDER BOOK CHECKLIST: PART ONE

More wonderful things for Wally fans to check out! Don't forget PART TWO at the end of this adventure!

ONCE UPON A PAGE . . .

- Helen of Troy and Paris
- Rudyard Kipling and the jungle book
- Sir Francis and his drake
- Wild Bill hiccup
- A shopping centaur
- Handel's water music
- George washing ton
- Samuel peeps at his diary
- Guy forks
- Tchaikovsky and the nut cracker sweet
- A Roundhead with a round head
- Pythagoras and the square of the hippopotamus
- William shakes spear
- Madame two swords
- Garibaldi and his biscuits
- Florence and her nightingale
- The pilgrim fathers
- Captain cook
- Hamlet making an omelette
- Jason and the juggernauts
- Whistling Whistler painting his mother
- Ali barber
- Lincoln and the Gettysburg address
- Stephenson's rocket
- Two knights fighting the war of the roses
- The Duke of Wellington's wellington

THE MIGHTY FRUIT FIGHT

- A box of dates next to a box of dates
- A pair of date palms
- "An apple a day keeps the doctor away!"
- Six crab apples
- Four naval oranges
- Blueberries wearing blue berets
- A kiwi fruit
- A banana doing the splits
- A pine apple
- Three fruit fools
- A bowl of fruit and a can of fruit
- Cranberry saws
- An orange upsetting the apple cart
- A banana tree
- Cooking apples
- Elder berry wine
- Seven wild cherries
- Goose berries
- A pound of apples
- A partridge in a pear tree
- A fruit cock tail
- Two peach halves
- "The Big Apple"
- One sour apple without a beard
- Paw paw fruit
- Another apple cart being upset

THE GAME OF GAMES

- Some stair cases
- Maize inside a maze
- A cross word
- A flight of stairs
- A map reading
- A player rolling the dice
- A tightrope walking
- A player with a map and a pair of compasses
- A player throwing a six
- One player not wearing gloves
- One lost glove
- The other lost glove
- A missing puzzle piece
- A bad mathematician
- Eight shovels
- Twenty-nine hoops
- Two pots of paint
- An upside down question mark on a player's tunic
- A blue player holding a green block
- A player with a magnet
- Five referees with their arms folded
- Five crying players with handkerchiefs
- Two players reading newspapers
- A smoke signal
- Three ticklish players
- Eight messages in bottles

TOYS! TOYS! TOYS!

- Two spinning tops and a top spinning
- Jack in the box
- A jack in a box
- A toy soldier being decorated
- A toy soldier in full dress uniform
- A toy drill sergeant
- A fish tank
- Two anchors
- A toy figure on skis
- A chalkboard
- A toy figure pushing a wheelbarrow
- A crow's nest
- An apple tree bookend
- A goal
- Five big red books
- A bear on a rocking horse
- A toy bandsman holding cymbals
- A toy performer balancing two chairs in the air
- Five wooden ladders
- A giraffe with a red-and-white-striped scarf
- A pirate carrying a barrel
- Toy figures climbing up a long scarf
- A teddy bear wearing a green scarf
- Two giraffes in the ark
- A robot holding a red tray

BRIGHT LIGHTS AND NIGHT FRIGHTS

- Street lights
- Lime light
- A rowing boat
- An octo-puss
- Moon light
- Light entertainers
- A very light house
- Day light
- A fishing boat
- A standard lamp
- Christmas tree lights
- A light weight boxer
- Star light
- A light at the end of the tunnel
- Stage lights
- A motor boat
- A sailor walking the plank
- A diving board
- Candle light
- A bedside light
- The deep blue C
- A Chinese lantern
- A search light
- A sleeping monster
- A mirror
- Four sailors looking through telescopes

THE CAKE FACTORY

- A loading bay
- Conveyor belts
- Two Danish pastries
- A gingerbread man
- Two workers blowing cream horns
- Maple syrup
- Hot cross buns
- A Viennese whirl
- A Swiss roll
- A pan cake
- A chocolate moose
- A custard-pie fight
- Apple pie
- Black forest gateau
- A fish cake
- Rock cakes
- Dough nuts
- A doe nut
- Baked Alaska pudding
- A fairy cake
- Mississippi mud pie
- Upside-down cake
- Carrot cake
- A cup of cake
- Sponge cakes
- A cake carrying a worker

ONCE UPON A PAGE...

HEY, WALLY FANS! LOOK AT ALL THESE BRILLIANT BOOKS! LOOK AT ALL THE CHARACTERS WHO HAVE STEPPED OUT FROM THEIR PAGES! WOW! WHAT A MAGIC SCENE! THESE BOOKS HAVE REALLY COME ALIVE! FANTASTIC — THAT BOOK OVER THERE IS ABOUT MY TRAVELS! AND WOOF, WENDA, WIZARD WHITEBEARD AND ODLAW ALL HAVE SPECIAL BOOKS OF THEIR OWN. NOW YOU CAN JOIN US TOO, IF YOU CAN FIND US, AND WE'LL TRAVEL TOGETHER THROUGH ALL THE OTHER WONDERFUL SCENES IN THIS WONDER BOOK. ONE SCENE IS MY SPECIAL FAVOURITE — YOU'LL NEVER GUESS WHAT MAKES IT SO GREAT. THE BOOKMARK MARKS IT, SO WHEN WE GET THERE, YOU WILL KNOW. NOW GET SEARCHING, WALLY FOLLOWERS, AND OFF WE GO! AND BE PREPARED FOR LOTS OF SURPRISES ALONG THE WAY!

Wally

THE SEARCH IS ON! FIND THESE FIVE INTREPID TRAVELLERS IN EVERY SCENE IN THE WONDER BOOK!

- FIND WALLY ... WHO TRAVELS EVERYWHERE!
- FIND WOOF ... WHO WAGS HIS TAIL! (WHICH IS ALL YOU CAN SEE)!
- FIND WENDA ... WHO TAKES THE PICTURES!
- FIND WIZARD WHITEBEARD ... WHO CASTS THE SPELLS!
- FIND ODLAW ... WHOSE GOOD DEEDS ARE FEW INDEED!

THE SEARCH CONTINUES! NEXT FIND THESE IMPORTANT THINGS THE TRAVELLERS HAVE LOST!

- FIND WALLY'S LOST KEY!
- FIND WOOF'S LOST BONE!
- FIND WENDA'S LOST CAMERA!
- FIND WIZARD WHITEBEARD'S MAGIC SCROLL!
- FIND ODLAW'S LOST BINOCULARS!

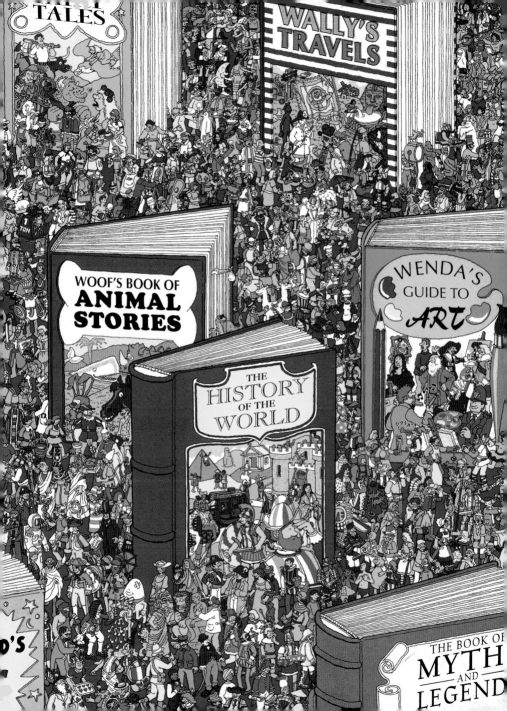

THE MIGHTY FRUIT FIGHT

WOW! AMAZING! HAVE YOU EVER IN YOUR LIVES SEEN A PLACE SO FULL OF FRUIT? HOW SWEET IT IS TO SAIL LEMON BOATS DOWN ORANGE JUICE RIVERS! BUT WATCH OUT, WALLY FANS! THE APPLES HAVE TURNED SOUR AND THEY'RE ATTACKING ALL THE OTHER FRUIT. WHOOSH! SQUIRT! SPLOOOOOSH! THERE'S A FRUIT JAM IN THE RIVER, SCUFFLES ON THE BANANA BRIDGES AND SUGAR BEING POURED ALL OVER THE STRAWBERRIES! PHEW! WHAT A MIGHTY FRUIT FIGHT!

THE GAME OF GAMES

STARTED! CAN YOU SPOT THE ONLY ORANGE TEAM PLAYER WHO HAS FINISHED? AND THE ONLY GREEN TEAM PLAYER WHO HAS NOT YET BEGUN?

FOUR HUGE TEAMS ARE PLAYING THIS GREAT GAME OF GAMES. THE REFEREES ARE TRYING TO SEE THAT NO ONE BREAKS THE RULES. BETWEEN THE STARTING-LINE AT THE TOP AND THE FINISHING-LINE AT THE BOTTOM, THERE ARE LOTS OF PUZZLES, BOOBY-TRAPS AND TESTS. THE GREEN TEAMS NEARLY WON, AND THE ORANGE TEAM'S HARDLY

TOYS! TOYS! TOYS!

WOW! ALL THE TEENY-TINY TOY CREATURES ARE COMING OUT OF THE TOYBOX TO EXPLORE THE PLAYROOM! THE BOOKS ARE TOO HUGE TO READ, BUT THE GREEN ONE IS PERFECT AS A FOOTBALL PITCH! SWOOSH! AND THE BOOK-MARK MAKES A BRILLIANT SLIDE! CAN YOU SEE A TEDDY TAKING OFF IN A PAPER PLANE? AND A DINOSAUR CHASING A CAVEMAN? WHAT HIGH JINKS AND HIGHWIRE ACTS ARE HAPPENING HERE! SO DO YOU THINK THAT THE TOYS ALWAYS HAVE GREAT TIMES LIKE THESE WHEN NO ONE IS ABOUT?

BRIGHT LIGHTS AND NIGHT FRIGHTS

HEY! WHAT BLAZING BEAMS OF LIGHT, WHAT A DAZZLING DISPLAY! GLITTER, TWINKLE, SPARKLE, FLASH – LOOK HOW BRIGHTLY THESE LIGHTHOUSES LIGHT UP THE NIGHT! BUT OH NO, THE MONSTERS WANT TO PUT THE LIGHTS OUT! THEY'RE ATTACKING FROM ALL SIDES. THE SAILORS ARE SQUIRTING PINK GUNGE AT THEM, BUT THE MONSTERS SPURT GREEN GUNGE RIGHT BACK! BUT WAIT! THREE OF THE MONSTERS ARE FIRING DIFFERENT COLOURED GUNGE! SPLASH, SPLAT, SPLURGE! CAN YOU SEE THEM, WALLY-WATCHERS?

THE CAKE FACTORY

MMMM! FEAST YOUR EYES, WALLY-WATCHERS! SNIFF THE DELICIOUS SMELLS OF BAKING CAKES! DROOL AT THE TASTY TOPPINGS! CAN YOU SEE A CAKE LIKE A TEAPOT, A CAKE LIKE A HOUSE, A CAKE SO TALL A WORKER ON THE FLOOR ABOVE IS LICKING IT? CAKES, CAKES, EVERYWHERE! HOW SCRUMPTIOUS! HOW YUM-YUM-YUMPTIOUS! LOOK

AT THE OOZING SUGAR ICING AND THE SHINY RED CHERRIES ON THE ROOF UP THERE! THAT ROOM IS WHERE THE FACTORY CONTROLLERS WORK, BUT HAVE THEY LOST CONTROL?

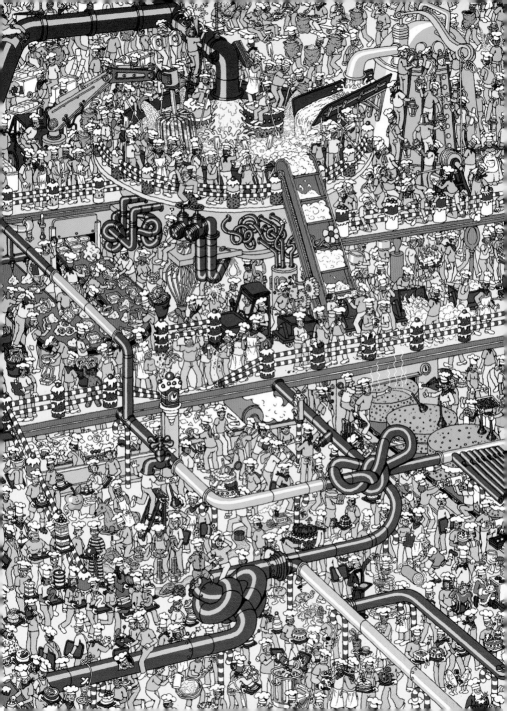

THE BATTLE OF THE BANDS

Boom, boom, rat-a-tat-tat! Have you ever heard such a beating of drums? Root-a-toot, tan-tara! Or such an ear-splitting blast of trumpets? A hostile army of bandsmen is massing beneath the ramparts of the Grand Castle of Music. Some are being pushed along in bandstands! Others are climbing music-note ladders! But what a strange thing! They are all dressed as animals! See the elephants, the bears, the crocs and the ducks! And just like their music they are wild and wacky!

THE ODLAW SWAMP

THE BRAVE ARMY OF MANY HATS IS TRYING TO GET THROUGH THIS FEARFUL SWAMP. HUNDREDS OF ODLAWS AND BLACK AND YELLOW SWAMP CREATURES ARE CAUSING TROUBLE IN THE UNDERGROWTH. THE REAL ODLAW IS THE ONE CLOSEST TO HIS LOST PAIR OF BINOCULARS. CAN YOU FIND HIM, X-RAY-EYED ONES? HOW MANY DIFFERENT KINDS OF HATS CAN YOU SEE ON THE SOLDIERS' HEADS? SQUELCH! SQUELCH! I'M GLAD I'M NOT IN THEIR SHOES! ESPECIALLY AS THEIR FEET ARE IN THE MURKY MUD!

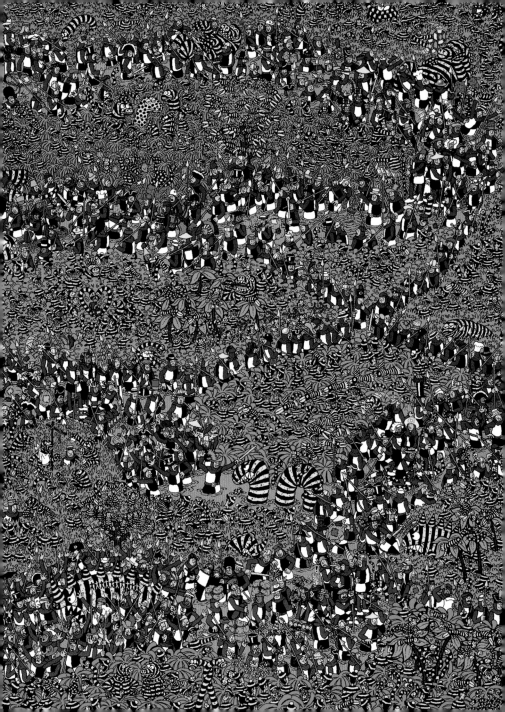

CLOWN TOWN

CLAP YOUR FEET, WALLY JOKERS! STAMP YOUR HANDS! YOU'LL GO OOGLY-BOOGLY-WOOGLY-EYED WITH WONDER! HERE ARE HUNDREDS OF CLOWNS PLAYING PRANKS AND MAKING MISCHIEF! LOOK AT THEIR COLOURFUL COSTUMES – WITH FLUFFY POMPOMS GALORE! AND THEIR BRIGHT AND SHINY NOSES! TOOT, TOOT! CAN YOU SEE A CAR WITH ITS TONGUE STICKING OUT?

TING-A-LING! AND A BIKE WITH SQUARE WHEELS? TEE, HEE! HA, HA! WHAT HAPPINESS IT IS TO BE IN CLOWN TOWN! SPLASH! SPLAT! EXCEPT FOR ALL THOSE SQUIRTY FLOWERS AND CUSTARD PIES!

THE FANTASTIC FLOWER GARDEN

WOW! WHAT A BRIGHT AND DAZZLING GARDEN SPECTACLE! ALL THE FLOWERS ARE IN FULL BLOOM, AND HUNDREDS OF BUSY GARDENERS ARE WATERING AND TENDING THEM. THE PETAL COSTUMES THEY ARE WEARING MAKE THEM LOOK LIKE FLOWERS THEMSELVES! VEGETABLES ARE GROWING IN THE GARDEN TOO. HOW MANY DIFFERENT KINDS

CAN YOU SEE? SNIFF THE AIR, WALLY FOLLOWERS! SMELL THE FANTASTIC SCENTS! WHAT A TREAT FOR YOUR NOSES AS WELL AS YOUR EYES!

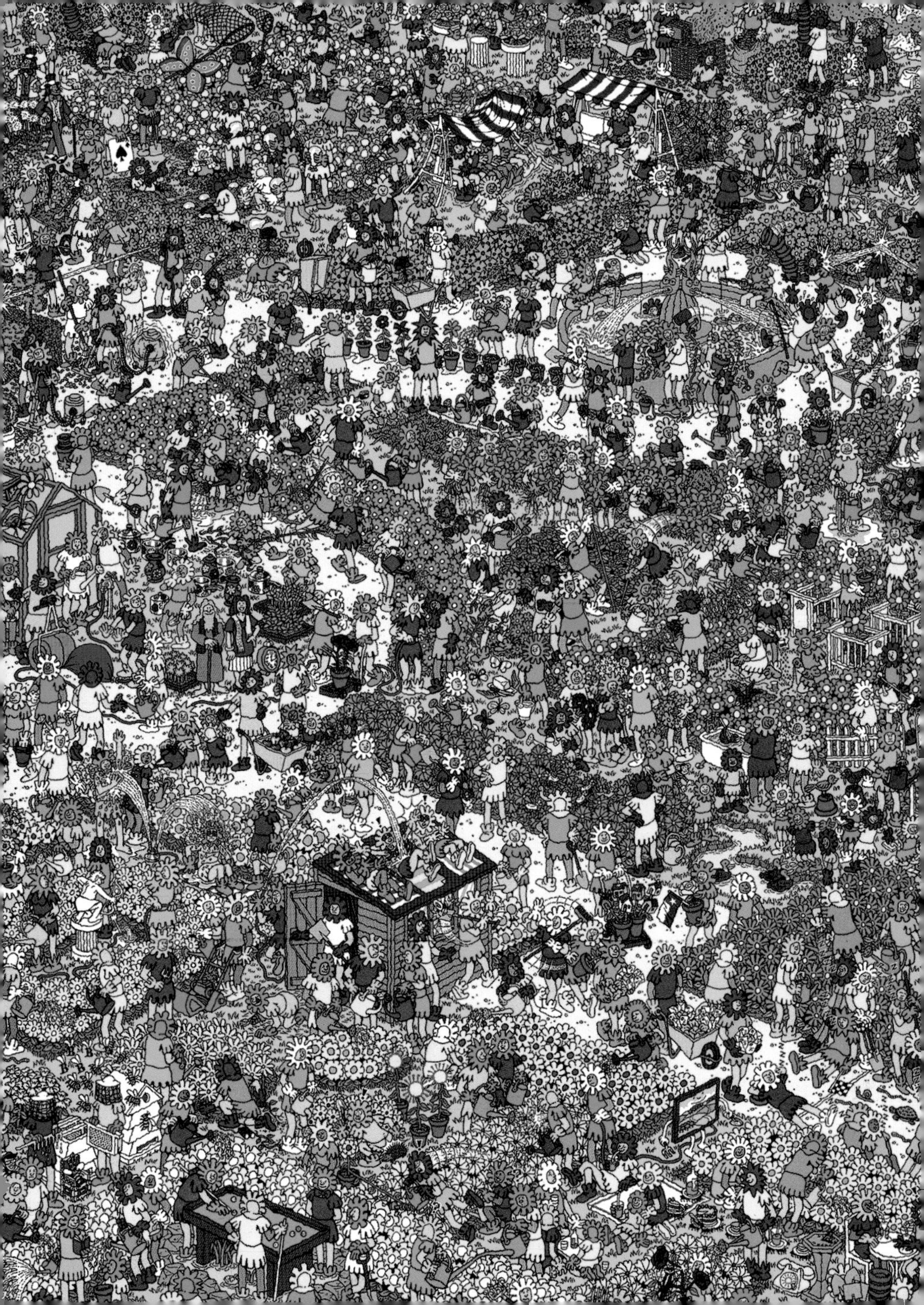

THE CORRIDORS OF TIME

TICK-TOCK, TICK-TOCK! THE HANDS OF ALL THE CLOCKS EXCEPT ONE SAY A QUARTER TO TWELVE. WHAT A DING-DONG THERE WILL BE WHEN THEY STRIKE! CAN YOU FIND THE ONLY CLOCK THAT TELLS A DIFFERENT TIME? IN THIS SCENE ARE THIRTY-SEVEN DOORS. ABOVE EACH DOOR APPEARS THE SHAPE OF THE KEY THAT WILL UNLOCK IT. CAN YOU FIND THE KEYS IN THE CROWD, BRAINY ONES, AND MATCH THEM TO THE SHAPES? OH NO! ONE DOOR HAS NO SHAPE ABOVE IT! EVEN SO YOU MUST FIND ITS KEY!

THE LAND
OF
WOOFS

HEY! LOOK AT ALL THESE DOGS THAT ARE
DRESSED LIKE WOOF! BOW, WOW, WOW! IN
THIS LAND, A DOG'S LIFE IS THE HIGH LIFE!
THERE'S A LUXURY WOOF HOTEL WITH A BONE-
SHAPED SWIMMING POOL, AND AT THE WOOF
RACE TRACK LOTS OF WOOFS ARE CHASING
ATTENDANTS DRESSED AS CATS, SAUSAGES
AND POSTMEN! THE BOOKMARK IS ON THIS
PAGE, WALLY FOLLOWERS, SO NOW YOU KNOW,
THIS IS MY FAVOURITE SCENE! THIS IS THE
ONLY SCENE IN THE BOOK WHERE YOU CAN
SEE MORE OF THE REAL WOOF THAN JUST
HIS TAIL! BUT CAN YOU FIND HIM? HE'S THE
ONLY ONE WITH FIVE RED STRIPES ON HIS
TAIL! HERE'S ANOTHER CHALLENGE! ELEVEN

TRAVELLERS HAVE FOLLOWED ME
HERE – ONE FROM EVERY SCENE. CAN
YOU SEE THEM? AND CAN YOU FIND
WHERE EACH ONE JOINED ME ON MY
ADVENTURES, AND SPOT ALL THEIR
APPEARANCES AFTERWARDS? KEEP
ON SEARCHING, WALLY FANS! HAVE
A WONDERFUL, WONDERFUL TIME!

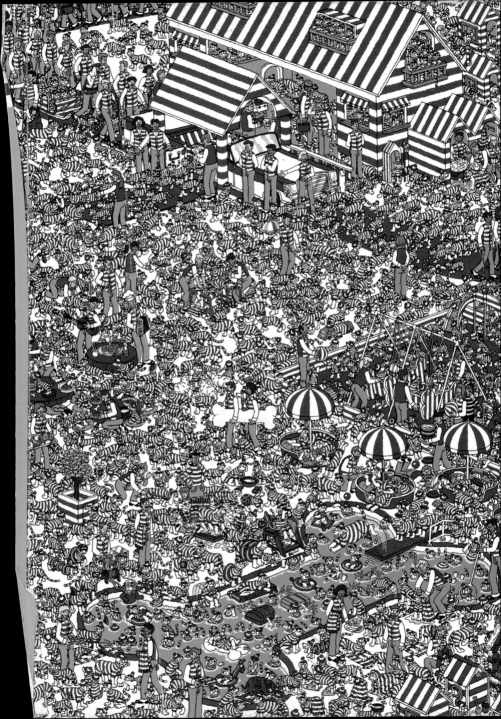

THE CORRIDORS OF TIME

- [ ] The clock striking twelve
- [ ] Wall clocks, clock faces and a clock tower
- [ ] An egg timer
- [ ] A very loud alarm clock
- [ ] A travelling clock
- [ ] A runner racing against time
- [ ] Roman numerals
- [ ] Time flies
- [ ] An hour glass
- [ ] Old Father Time and Big Ben
- [ ] Grandfather clocks
- [ ] A walking stick
- [ ] Thirty-six pairs of almost identical twins
- [ ] One pair of identical twins
- [ ] A man's braces being pulled in opposite directions
- [ ] A swinging pendulum
- [ ] Coat tails tied in a knot
- [ ] A door and thirteen clocks on their sides
- [ ] A very tall top hat
- [ ] A sundial
- [ ] A pair of hooked umbrellas
- [ ] A clock cuckoo
- [ ] A pair of tangled walking sticks

THE BATTLE OF THE BANDS

- [ ] A rubber band
- [ ] A piano forty
- [ ] A pipe band
- [ ] Bandsmen "playing" their instruments
- [ ] A fan fair
- [ ] Bandsmen with saxophones and sacks of phones
- [ ] A steel band
- [ ] A swing band
- [ ] Sheet music
- [ ] Racing bandsmen "beating" their drums
- [ ] A rock band
- [ ] Kettle drums
- [ ] A mouth organ
- [ ] A baby sitar
- [ ] A 1-man band
- [ ] A French horn
- [ ] A barrel organ
- [ ] Some violin bows
- [ ] A rock and roll band
- [ ] Bandsmen playing cornets
- [ ] A drummer with drum sticks
- [ ] A big elephant trunk
- [ ] Bandsmen making a drum kit
- [ ] The orchestra pit
- [ ] A bag piper
- [ ] Some cheetah bandsmen cheating

THE ODLAW SWAMP

- [ ] Two soldiers disguised as Odlaws
- [ ] A soldier wearing a bowler hat
- [ ] A soldier wearing a stovepipe hat
- [ ] A soldier wearing a riding helmet
- [ ] A soldier wearing a straw hat
- [ ] Three soldiers wearing peaked caps
- [ ] A lady wearing an Easter bonnet
- [ ] Two soldiers wearing American football helmets
- [ ] Two soldiers wearing baseball caps
- [ ] A big shield next to a little shield
- [ ] A lady wearing a sun hat
- [ ] A soldier with two big feathers in his hat
- [ ] Some rattle snakes
- [ ] Five romantic snakes
- [ ] Seven wooden rafts
- [ ] Three small wooden boats
- [ ] Four birds' nests
- [ ] One Odlaw in disguise
- [ ] A swamp creature without stripes
- [ ] A monster cleaning its teeth
- [ ] A monster asleep, but not for long
- [ ] A soldier floating on a parcel
- [ ] A very big monster with a very small head
- [ ] One charmed snake
- [ ] Five charmed spears
- [ ] A snake reading

CLOWN TOWN

- [ ] A clown reading a newspaper
- [ ] A starry umbrella
- [ ] A clown with a blue teapot
- [ ] Two hoses leaking
- [ ] A clown with two hoops on each arm
- [ ] A clown looking through a telescope
- [ ] Two clowns holding big hammers
- [ ] A clown with a bag of crackers
- [ ] Two clowns holding flowerpots
- [ ] A clown swinging a pillow
- [ ] A clown combing the roof of a Clown Town house
- [ ] A clown bursting a balloon
- [ ] Six flowers squirting the same clown
- [ ] A clown wearing a jack-in-the-box hat
- [ ] Three cars
- [ ] Three watering cans
- [ ] A clown with a fishing rod
- [ ] One hat joining two clowns
- [ ] A clown about to catapult a custard pie
- [ ] Clowns wearing tea shirts
- [ ] Three clowns with buckets of water
- [ ] A clown with a yo-yo
- [ ] A clown stepping into a custard pie
- [ ] Seventeen clouds
- [ ] A clown having his foot tickled
- [ ] One clown with a green-coloured nose

THE FANTASTIC FLOWER GARDEN

- [ ] The yellow rose of Texas
- [ ] Flower pots and flower beds
- [ ] Butter flies
- [ ] Gardeners sowing seeds and planting bulbs
- [ ] A garden nursery
- [ ] A bird bath and a bird table
- [ ] House plants, wall flowers and blue bells
- [ ] Dandy lions, tiger lilies and fox gloves
- [ ] Cabbage patches, letters leaves and a collie flower
- [ ] A hedgehog next to a hedge hog
- [ ] A flower border and a flower show
- [ ] A bull frog
- [ ] Earth worms
- [ ] A wheelbarrow full of wheels
- [ ] A cricket match
- [ ] Parsley, sage, Rosemary and time
- [ ] A queen bee near a honey comb
- [ ] A landscape gardener
- [ ] A sun dial next to a sundial
- [ ] Gardeners dancing to the beetles
- [ ] A green house and a tree house
- [ ] A spring onion and a leek with a leak
- [ ] Door mice
- [ ] An apple tree
- [ ] Weeping willows and climbing roses
- [ ] Rock pool

THE LAND OF WOOFS

- [ ] Dog biscuits
- [ ] A mountain dog
- [ ] A hot dog getting cool
- [ ] A gray hound bus
- [ ] Dog baskets
- [ ] A pair of swimming trunks
- [ ] A sheep dog
- [ ] A watch dog
- [ ] A bull dog
- [ ] A great Dane
- [ ] A guard dog
- [ ] A dog in a wet suit
- [ ] Some swimming costumes
- [ ] A dog with a red collar
- [ ] A dog wearing a yellow collar with a blue disc
- [ ] A dog with a blue bobble on his hat
- [ ] A top dog
- [ ] A sausage dog with sausages
- [ ] A dog wearing a blue collar with a green disc
- [ ] A cat dressed like a Woof dog
- [ ] The puppies' pool
- [ ] A dog doing a paw stand
- [ ] A Scottie dog
- [ ] Two dogs having a massage
- [ ] A sniffer dog
- [ ] Twenty-two red-and-white striped towels

★ CLOWNING AROUND! ★

Ha, ha! What a joker! The clown who follows Wally and his friends to the end of the book changes the colour of his hatband in one scene! Can you find which scene it is? What colour does his hatband change to?

This edition published 2008 by Walker Books Ltd
87 Vauxhall Walk, London SE11 5HJ

6 8 10 9 7 5